Microsoft Access 2010
Tutorial and Lab Manual

David Murray
University at Buffalo

Kendall Hunt
publishing company

Microsoft Access 2010 Tutorial and Lab Manual is an independent textbook and is not affiliated with, nor has it been authorized, sponsored, or otherwise approved by Microsoft Corporation.

Cover image © Shutterstock, Inc.

Kendall Hunt
publishing company

www.kendallhunt.com
Send all inquiries to:
4050 Westmark Drive
Dubuque, IA 52004-1840

ISBN 978-0-7575-8940-9

Printed in the United States of America

10 9 8 7 6 5 4 3

This book is dedicated to my loving wife Amy
and my precious daughter Giacinta.

CONTENTS

PREFACE

Are You Ready to Learn Microsoft Access?

Many students find learning a brand new technology to be an overwhelming and often confusing and frustrating experience. If you are intimidated by Microsoft Access, take heart! Let me assure you that no matter how little experience you have or how much you hate computers (or they hate you), **you CAN learn this software program with a little work, time, and dedication.**

This book is written so that you will learn the fundamentals of Microsoft Access in a step-by-step and hands-on fashion. The hands-on walkthrough and applied practice is what makes this textbook "work," but that is only half of the formula to make your learning effective. There must also be a commitment from you, the reader, to take an active and engaged role in the learning process. Specifically, while you are reading and working through this book, do so in a deliberate manner, paying careful attention to what is being explained. Blindly pointing and clicking through the exercises without thinking about the material being covered will not result in effective learning of the software.

I hope that this book will provide you with the foundational knowledge to comfortably work with Microsoft Access databases. There is so much you can do in Microsoft Access that is beyond the scope of this textbook, and this foundation will ultimately help you **independently learn** how to do advanced things with the software. As with most books, this book can provide only limited depth into the material. Your true learning will begin after you have mastered the basics in this textbook and start attempting to use the software in real-world applications.

Good luck!

Overview of Microsoft Access Databases

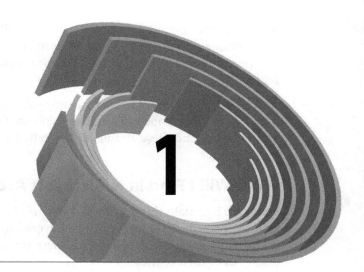

Introduction

This first introductory chapter will provide you with a broad overview of Microsoft Access and will introduce you to some general database terminology used throughout the book. This is accomplished by looking at Access databases from an end-user perspective so that you can familiarize yourself with what databases are, what they contain, and in general how they are used. Subsequent chapters focus on the technical details of databases, and by the end of this book, the topics come full circle in an attempt to tie together all of the concepts covered in this book.

Each chapter begins with a brief textual overview of the material, followed by a Guided Exercise, which takes you step-by-step through a hands-on database example of the chapter contents. At the conclusion of most chapters, you have the opportunity to complete an Applied Exercise to check your knowledge and application of the material learned. Adhering to the chapter readings and paying attention to the "Guided Exercises" should prepare you to successfully complete the Applied Exercises, which are a true test of the material you have learned.

Have You Ever Used a Database?

If you are learning Microsoft Access for the first time, you may instinctively answer "no" to the question of whether you have ever used a database. I'm absolutely positive, however, that you have interacted with many databases, whether you realize it or not. To understand this, let's examine what the term **database** truly means by listing some basic characteristics of databases.

- Databases store all kinds of data.
- Databases are either low-tech (manual) or high-tech (electronic).
- Databases are highly structured and organized.
- Databases are somewhat analogous to multiple spreadsheets that are linked together.
- Databases are designed to allow easy extraction and use of the stored data.

So, if you have ever used a phone book or a library card catalog, you have indeed used a database. Also, many online search engines and e-commerce websites rely on databases for their proper functioning, so you likely have interacted with them. **See, you may already be more familiar with databases than you realize!**

Although the concept of a database may still seem foreign and new to you, it is helpful to relate the material in this book to examples of databases you are familiar with. Doing so will often help you to demystify and better understand these strange things called databases.

What Will I Find in a Microsoft Access Database?

There are five main things (objects) you will find in an Access database: tables, queries, forms, reports, and macros. Each of these topics will be covered in greater detail throughout the subsequent chapters. Take a minute to familiarize yourself with these terms. The Guided Exercise later in this chapter will show you examples of each of these.

1. **Tables** store the data in the database and are analogous to the foundation of the database. It is critically important that the tables be designed properly; they provide the foundation for building the remainder of the database.

2. **Queries** enable you to extract data from your database tables and allow us to answer questions we have about the data. Queries may combine data from multiple tables and manipulate data output through the use of expressions, formulas, and functions.

3. **Forms** are based on tables or queries, and they are used for entering data into the database in a user-friendly manner. They are also used for displaying data to the end user and can be used to create a menu system for the database.

4. **Reports** use data from a table or query and format the output in a professional-looking manner. Reports provide you with the ability to summarize, sort, group, and display the data in many different ways suited to the needs of the end user. Often, the purpose of a report is to provide a printed output of some data in your database.

5. **Macros** are small programs that you build into Microsoft Access; they perform some advanced operations, making the database more user-friendly and/or functional.

Where Can I Get Help?

F1. Simply, press the F1 key in Microsoft Access to use the built-in help anytime you need it. You should also use the numerous online resources that are available.

Aside from the Applied Exercises at the conclusion of some chapters, nothing in this book is intended to be extraordinarily difficult or challenging to complete. If you find yourself stuck on a step of a Guided Exercise, try re-reading a few steps back to see if you either missed something or misunderstood the instructions. It is important to read each step carefully and follow the directions closely.

Chapter 1 Guided Exercise

1. Download the **StudentRoster.accdb** file from the course website. After you click on the filename on the website, you will have to select either the "Save" or "Save to Disk" option depending on the web browser you are using. **Do NOT choose the Open option.** You should save the file to your desktop, flash drive, or other convenient location.

2. After downloading the file, navigate to where it is stored on your computer. Double-click the **StudentRoster.accdb** file to open it in Microsoft Access 2010. If you do not have the 2010 version of Microsoft Access installed, it may not open the database file.

3. Next, click the **Enable Content** button that appears toward the top of the database. The following screenshot illustrates what you should look for. If instead you see an **Options** button, you are using Access 2007. Please **STOP** and install Access 2010.

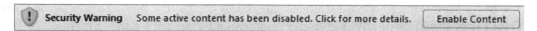

You will have to click the **Enable Content** button the very first time you open a database file. It will also display the first time you open a file after it has been moved to another location or renamed.

4. Once the database file opens, you will see a list of the database objects (tables, queries, forms, reports, macros) in a panel called the Navigation Pane, which appears on the left side of the database. On the right side, you will see a menu system that was developed specifically for this database example.

5. Click on the drop-down list shown in the following screenshot to ensure you have both the **Object Type** and **All Access Objects** options selected to display.

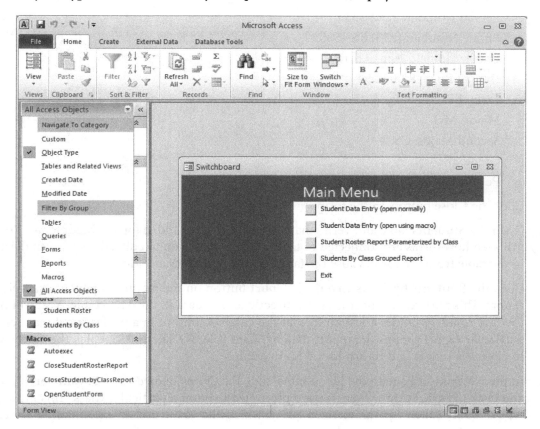

6. To begin looking at examples of these database objects, double-click the table named **Students** to open it. You should see a few records of data already in the table.

7. Add a new record for yourself in the table. You can do this by entering your data below the last record in the table. Make sure you add your name, person number, email, phone number, date of birth, class, major, second major (optional), grade, and performance. **As you navigate from record to record, Access automatically saves any data entry changes that have been made.**

8. Find the record for Susan Ward and change her name from **Ward, Susan** to **Ward, Sue.** As you make this edit, you will see that it is very simple to make changes to data in the database tables.

9. Close the table by clicking on the LOWER X in the upper right-hand corner of the database. Clicking the UPPER X will close the entire database instead of just the table. It is a common mistake, and you will likely close the entire database accidentally at least a few times while working through this book.

10. The Main Menu should be visible once again. Click on the first menu button named **Student Data Entry (open normally)** to see an example of a form used for data entry.

11. View the various data records on the form using the navigation buttons at the bottom of the form. This form is built off of the **Students** table.

12. Click on the **Student Name** control so it is selected and then click the **Find Record** button to see if you can find your record in the database. You may have to adjust the search options on the **Find and Replace** window in order to find your record.

13. Click the **Add Record** button and add the following data.

    Student Name: Duffield, Ryan
    Person Number: 2222-3333
    Phone Number: (555) 867-5309
    Email: rduffield@email.com
    Date of Birth: 8/20/1994
    Class: FR
    Major: MG
    Second Major: CS
    Grade: B
    Performance: Satisfactory

14. Click the **Close** button on the form.

15. Open the **Students** table and verify that a record has been added for **Duffield, Ryan.** You have just seen how forms are connected to tables, which allow you to edit, add, and even delete data in the table from the form. Close the table to return to the Main Menu.

16. Click the **Students by Class Grouped Report** button on the menu to open an example of a report. This particular report is based directly on the data in the MGS table. You will notice that the report provides a way to format the database output in a professional manner. This particular report groups the report data by Class (FR, SO, JR, or SR). Click the **Close** button to close the report and return to the Main Menu.

17. In the Navigation Pane to the left, double-click the Query named **ClassParameter.** Type **JR** and click the **OK** button when you are prompted to enter a particular Class. This is a special type of query called a parameterized query, which allows the user to enter in different criterion each time the query is executed.

18. To see how the parameter works, close the query results (click the LOWER X), double-click **ClassParameter** again to reopen it, and enter **FR.** This time, different data results will be returned. Parameterized queries are powerful and quite easy to develop in Access, as you will learn later in Chapter 4. Close the query results to return to the Main Menu.

19. We will come back to the query in just a second, but first, open the **Students** table and switch the class for Duffield, Ryan from **FR** to **SR.** Next, close the table, and reopen the **ClassParameter** query. This time enter **SR** when prompted for a Class. You should see that the record for Duffield, Ryan is now included in this query result. This demonstrates an important point: **each time a query is executed, it is connecting to the table to get the most recent data.** Close the query results to return to the Main Menu.

20. Reports can be built from tables or queries. Click the **Student Roster Report Parameterized by Class** button on the Main Menu to display a report based on the **ClassParameter** query introduced previously. When prompted for a Class, enter **SR.**

    You are prompted to enter a Class, because every time the report is run, it also executes the query the report is based on. This always results in the query retrieving the most up-to-date data from the table and displaying those results in the report. Click the **Close** button to close the report and return to the Main Menu.

21. The final database object for you to explore are macros. The Main Menu that automatically appeared when you first opened the database was controlled with a special macro named **Autoexec.** Any macro saved with this name will be automatically executed when the database is opened. Often, you will use this macro to open your Main Menu so that the database users have access to their forms and reports.

22. Another example of a macro can be demonstrated by clicking on the **Student Data Entry (open using macro)** button on the Main Menu. Watch and read the pop-up windows carefully as they describe step-by-step what this particular macro is doing. Click the **Close Form** button to return to the Main Menu.

23. Before exiting the database entirely, click on the **File** ribbon in the upper left-hand corner of Access and click the **Compact & Repair Database** button. You will notice that the database closes and reopens quickly when this option is selected.

24. The **Compact & Repair Database** option is very important to know about in Access. Access database files are unique because **they will never shrink in size** and will only get larger! As you add and remove items to a database over time, it will become much larger and "bloated" in size. Running the **Compact & Repair Database** option will shrink the database to its smallest size. Although it is not necessary to do this every time when finished with a database, you will find it useful to run periodically.

25. Click the **Exit** button on the Main Menu to exit the database.

Throughout the Chapter 1 Guided Exercise, you have had the opportunity to see examples of tables, forms, queries, reports, and macros **from the end-user perspective.** Throughout the next six chapters, we will dig deeper into each of these topics and explore how these database objects are created "from scratch." Before continuing, make sure you have, at a minimum, a general understanding of the five database objects covered in this chapter.

Design and
Create Tables
to Store Data

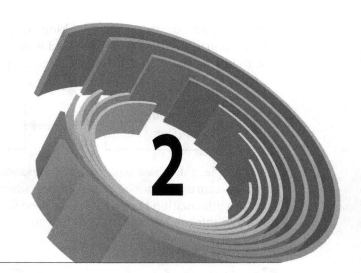

2

Introduction

In the introductory chapter, you had an opportunity to explore and learn about databases from the end-user perspective. In addition, you discovered that Microsoft Access databases are composed of objects called tables, forms, queries, reports, and macros. If you have not completed the Guided Exercise in Chapter 1, it is strongly recommended that you do so before continuing in order to familiarize yourself with the database objects.

This book devotes a chapter to each database object, with this chapter beginning a detailed look at **tables.** Here is the description of database tables provided in Chapter 1.

- "Tables store the data in the database and are analogous to the foundation of the database. It is critically important that the tables be designed properly; they provide the foundation for building the remainder of the database."

Throughout portions of this chapter, a construction analogy is used to describe databases and tables because designing and building a database shares similarities with designing and building a house. In addition to learning about the specific properties and settings for tables, some basic table design principles to follow will be introduced. You will begin by exploring what databases are used for, which gives insight into how they should be properly designed and constructed.

Decisions, Decisions, Decisions!

We constantly make decisions. Some are big, some are small, some are conscious, and some are subconscious. But **every single one of them has some impact.** In the same way, managers and employees of a business make many decisions every single day that affect the profitability of the business. Ideally, we want managers and their employees to make the best possible decisions that will benefit the business. One way to achieve this is to provide employees with timely and good information to help them with their daily decision making.

By their nature, **databases are well suited for providing information that supports decision making.** As explained in Chapter 1, "Databases are designed to allow easy extraction and use of the stored data."

In other words, databases store all kinds of data, allowing us to later process the stored data into useful information. Once data is transformed into information, it can then be used to support decision making. The following diagram illustrates this principle of data being processed into information to be used in decision making.

For example, a database with tens of thousands of records is essentially useless if we have to pore through the data records one by one. In contrast, when we summarize, filter, group, and/or sort the data, it then becomes information because it can be used for business and managerial decision making. To be successful in today's information age, businesses must act on good information in a timely fashion.

Garbage In, Garbage Out

To make good decisions, **it is important to have good information based on good data.** Allowing incorrect, incomplete, or inconsistent (bad) data into a database will usually result in incorrect information being generated. This is described with the basic computing principle of GIGO (garbage in, garbage out), which explains how computers and databases treat bad data. As much as possible, we want to avoid GIGO because the database does not automatically discern whether the data are "good" or "bad."

Designing database tables properly is one way to help ensure that only good data make their way into the database. As a result, we can be fairly confident that the good data can be processed into good information, and hopefully, good decisions will follow.

How Do You Properly Design the Foundation?

The most important part of any building is the foundation. It is extremely important that a structure have a good foundation; otherwise, the structure may fall, shift, crack, and ultimately fail. In the same way, a database must have a solid foundation or it too will fail. The tables of a database are likened to the foundation because everything else is built upon them. As much as possible, you want to create the tables only once and limit changes to them after work begins on the remainder of the database. Making drastic design changes to the tables may result in having to rebuild other portions of the database.

Although this chapter does not cover the advanced topic of relational database design, we still need to keep in mind good database design principles. **I cannot emphasize enough that proper database design is critically important to the success of a database system!** Following these four principles will help ensure that your database has a solid foundation and will lessen the possibility of "bad" data making their way into your database.

1. **Do not store redundant data in the database tables.**

   Why? Data stored more than once in your database makes updating data difficult and often leads to inconsistent (bad) data.

2. **Do not store calculated or derived data in database tables.**

   Why? Calculated or derived data should not be stored because the values used in the calculation may change, which would also require an update of the calculated data. In addition, calculations based on time would eventually result in inaccurate data being stored in the table.

Consider the option of storing the age or date of birth of an employee in a table. If you choose to store age, within a year, all the data will be incorrect in the table unless it is constantly updated! Instead, you should store date of birth, which does not change. But how then would you display the age of an employee on a report if only the date of birth is stored in the table? There are two options. First, **you can always build a query to generate a calculated value instead of having to store it in a table.**

The second option, new to Access 2010, is to create a field in the table with the Calculated data type. This is particularly useful when the calculated data is used in multiple forms and reports since you only have to create it one time in the table. Also, while this second approach appears to directly contradict the principle of not storing calculated data, it is perfectly valid to use this special data type in Microsoft Access.

3. **Ensure that data are stored in their smallest parts in the table.**

   Why? I'll explain by example: storing employee name in one column of a table makes sorting or searching on that column very difficult. Instead, split the employee name into first name and last name to make the table data easier to use and more flexible.

4. **Reporting needs should determine the data stored in the tables.**

   Why? Although this one is self-explanatory, it is a good reminder that the outputs of the database (reports) should determine what data need to be stored in the database tables. Failure to include necessary data in your tables will result in incomplete outputs.

How Do You Properly Build the Foundation?

Now that you have some context to understand how tables are designed and what they are used for, let's dive in and explore some technical details and basic terminology you will need to understand.

Tables are composed of **fields** (vertical columns) and **records** (horizontal rows), and they are used to store data in a highly structured and organized format. Each field is assigned a name that explains the type of data stored in that column. For example, in a table storing retail store locations for a company, you may find fields for LocationName, Address, City, State, Zip, and Phone. If there are 65 retail store locations across the United States, then there would be 65 records in the table: one record for each location.

You can examine a table in Microsoft Access either in the **Datasheet View** or the **Design View.** As you saw in the Chapter 1 Guided Exercise, the Datasheet View is used to work with, enter, and delete data. In addition, you can sort, format, filter, find, and summarize the data in the Datasheet View.

The Design View was not discussed in the Chapter 1 Guided Exercise because most end users of the database system will not work in the Design View of the table. This view is the "behind-the-scenes" view where the underlying structure of the table is created. While working in the Design View, you can modify the fields, their data types, and their properties. It is important to properly set the data type and properties of each field to help prevent bad data from being entered into your database tables. Additionally, you can create very powerful **Data Macros** to further validate record updates or new data entry. Data Macros can also be used to trigger other events such as creating a separate audit log, sending email notifications, or updating related data records.

In general, a **data type** defines the type of the data that are going to be stored in that particular field. The valid data types in Microsoft Access databases are Text, Memo, Number, Date/Time, Currency, Auto Number, Yes/No, OLE Object, Hyperlink, and Attachment. Calculated and Lookup Wizard are two special data types that are also valid.

- **Text** stores up to 255 characters of text, numbers, and symbols.
- **Memo** stores up to 63,999 characters of text, numbers, and symbols.

- **Number** stores numbers that are used in mathematical calculations. You should *not* use this type to store data such as zip codes because zip code data are not used for mathematical calculations. Instead, use a Text data type for zip code fields and any other fields that have numbers in them but are not used in mathematical calculations (Social Security number, phone number, student person number, etc.).

- **Date/Time** stores dates and times.

- **Currency** stores currency values up to four decimal places.

- **AutoNumber** automatically assigns a unique number to each record. This assignment can be done sequentially or randomly.

- **Yes/No** stores any binary representation of data such as Yes or No, True or False, or On or Off. A field with this data type appears as a checkbox in the Datasheet view.

- **OLE Object** stores or links to an object such as a Microsoft Word document, an image file, or a Microsoft Excel spreadsheet. It is recommended that you use the new Attachment data type instead of the OLE Object data type.

- **Hyperlink** stores website addresses, email addresses, and hyperlink data.

- **Attachment** stores various file formats in the database with the option of editing files within the database.

- **Calculated** is a brand-new and special data type in Access 2010. It is used to display results of calculations or expressions based on other fields in the table. The results of a calculated field are read-only.

- **Lookup Wizard** is technically not a data type, but it does appear in the data type list because it easily enables you to create a drop-down list (combo box) of values that the user can select from in the table. This list of values can be typed in manually or dynamically based on another table in the database. This feature makes data entry easier for the end user and can help eliminate bad data from being entered into the database.

Depending on the data type, each field also has specific properties that can be set. Although the following list of properties is not exhaustive, remember that you can always click F1 to get help about a specific property you encounter using Microsoft Access. Included here are some of the common properties used for a Text field.

- **Field Size** sets the maximum number of characters that can be entered for this field. For Text data types, the maximum value is 255 characters. Generally, this should be set as small as possible but large enough to accommodate potentially large entries of data.

- **Format** adjusts how the data are displayed as output. For Date/Time data types, this will adjust the date and time format used. For Number data types, this provides the option to select from Fixed, Standard, Percent, Scientific, or General Number formats. Different settings are also available for Text, Currency, and Yes/No data types.

- **Input Mask** creates a predefined structure into which the data for this field must be entered. Phone number and Social Security number fields commonly use Input Masks because the data follow a set structure every time.

- **Caption** provides an alternative field name to be displayed on all database objects that reference this field. For example, in a field named SSN, you may enter Social Security number as the Caption. Captions are used to display more descriptive field names to the end user.

- **Default Value** Automatically adds this set value for property to each new record in the table. This can be useful for reducing data entry when a large percentage of records use the same field data.

- **Validation Rule** is a property that works in conjunction with the Validation Text described next. The Validation Rule property enables you to set specific data entry rules that must be strictly followed. For example, you can force the users to enter data in a prespecified list or range of data.

- **Validation Text** is the text displayed in the error or warning message that appears when data entered into the database violate the corresponding Validation Rule.

- **Required,** when selected, forces the end user to enter data into this field before continuing to another record. Make sure this is enforced only when you need this field data 100% of the time. If there are situations when the data may not be available or do not exist, it is advised not to enforce this property.

One final, but very important, option to set in the Design View of a table is the **primary key.** A primary key is a field or combination of fields that uniquely identifies a record in a table. **Every table in a database must have a primary key established.**

To understand primary keys, consider an example of a database table containing a list of vehicles registered for on-campus parking at a university. The fields in the table are VIN, Make, Model, Color, LicensePlate, LicenseState, RegistrationDate, and VehicleType, and each record in the table is a separate vehicle. Given this example, the following are three ways you can set a primary key in the table.

1. **Use an existing field that uniquely identifies each record in the table.**

   Example: Use Vehicle Identification Number (VIN).

2. **Create a new field to act as the primary key and assign it the AutoNumber data type.**

   Example: Add a field named VehicleID and set the data type to AutoNumber.

3. **Combine multiple fields to create a concatenated primary key.**

   Example: Use both LicensePlate and LicenseState as a concatenated key.

At least one of these three approaches can always be used for establishing a primary key in any table you encounter. The easiest method is to add a new field to the table and set it to the AutoNumber data type.

Chapter 2 Guided Exercise

1. Download the **Employees.accdb** file from the course website. After you click on the filename on the website, you will have to select either the "Save" or "Save to Disk" option depending on the web browser you are using. **Do NOT choose the Open option.** You should save the file to your desktop, flash drive, or other convenient location.

2. After downloading the file, navigate to where it is stored on your computer. Double-click the **Employees.accdb** file to open it in Microsoft Access 2010.

3. Next, click the **Enable Content** button that appears toward the top of the database. The following screenshot illustrates what you should look for. If instead you see an **Options** button, you are using Access 2007. Please **STOP** and install Access 2010.

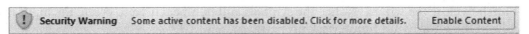

   You will have to click the **Enable Content** button the very first time you open a database file. It will also display the first time you open a file after it has been moved to another location or renamed.

4. Click on the drop-down list above the Navigation Pane to ensure you have both the **Object Type** and **All Access Objects** options selected to display. This is illustrated with a screenshot in the Chapter 1 Guided Exercise if you need help with this step.

5. Double-click the **Employees** table to open it in Datasheet View and add a sample record for your Teaching Assistant in the table. You can do this by entering the data below the last record. Use the correct first and last name of your TA. The rest of the data record for your TA should be made up.

6. Select the **Home** ribbon and click on the **View** button in the upper left-hand corner to switch to the Design View of the table. The **View** button icon is a picture of a pencil, ruler, and triangle.

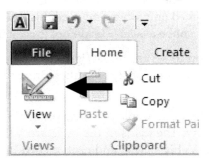

7. Click on the various fields in the Design View. As you do this, briefly examine the different properties for each field.

8. Click on the **View** button in the upper left-hand corner (it looks different now) to switch back to the Datasheet View of the table. The **View** button is an easy way to toggle back and forth between the Datasheet and Design View of a table. Click once more on the **View** button to switch back to the Design View of the Employees table.

9. Click on the **EmployeeID** field to select it. Select the **Design** ribbon and click on the **Primary Key** button. A small picture of a key appears next to EmployeeID; this indicates that the field has been set as the primary key.

10. Beneath the **PhoneNum** field, add a field named **Email.** Set the data type to **Hyperlink.** Set the **Caption** property for this field to **Email Address.**

11. Add another field named **Salary** and set the data type as **Currency.** Set the **Validation Rule** property for this field to >=**20000.** Set the **Validation Text** property for this field to **Enter a salary above $20,000.**

12. Add another field named **HireDate** and set the data type as **Date/Time.** Set the **Format** property for this field to **Short Date.**

13. Click the **PhoneNum** field to select it. Click the **Input Mask** property. A build button ⬚ (small button with three dots) should appear to the right of the **Input Mask** row. Click the build button to open the **Input Mask Wizard.** Click **Yes** if prompted to Save the table.

   Click **Yes** if prompted with the message, "**Data integrity rules have been changed; existing data may not be valid for the new rules.**" Click **Yes** if prompted with the message, "**Existing data violates the new setting for the 'Validation Rule' property for field 'Salary'**".

14. Select the Input Mask for phone number and click **Next.** Click **Next** twice more and then click **Finish** to close the wizard. Notice the symbols and numbers used to create the input mask are now in the PhoneNum Input Mask property.

15. With the Input Mask property selected, Press **F1** to open the help system and look at the different characters and symbols that can be used to create a custom input mask. Close the help system and return to the Design View of the Employees tables.

16. Click the **State** field to select it. Click the **Default Value** property and set it to **NY.** Set the **Field Size** property to **2.**

17. Click the **City** field to select it. Change the data type from Text to **Lookup Wizard.**

18. Select the radio button labeled "**I will type in the values that I want.**" Click **Next.**

19. Enter **Amherst** in the first row under Col1. Enter **Buffalo** below Amherst. Enter **Clarence** below Buffalo. Click **Next.** Click **Finish.**

20. Click the **City** field to select it. Click the **Lookup** tab in the **Field Properties** section.

General	Lookup	
Display Control	Combo Box
Row Source Type	Value List
Row Source	"Amherst";"Buffalo";"Clarence"
Bound Column	1
Column Count	1
Column Heads	No
Column Widths	1"
List Rows	16
List Width	1"
Limit To List	Yes
Allow Multiple Values	No
Allow Value List Edits	No
List Items Edit Form	
Show Only Row Source V	No

21. Set the **Limit to List** property to **Yes** as indicated in the preceding screenshot. This setting will only allow the data in the combo box to be added to the City field. Click on the **General** tab.

22. Click the **City** field to select it. Click the **Required** property and set it to **Yes.** Click the **Allow Zero Length** property and set it to **No.**

    Click the **View** button to switch back to the Datasheet View of the table. Click **Yes** if prompted to Save the table. Click **Yes** if prompted with the message, "**Some data may be lost.**" Click **Yes** if prompted with the message, "**Data integrity rules have been changed; existing data may not be valid for the new rules.**"

23. Add a new record for yourself in the table. You can do this by entering your data below the last record in the table. Make sure you add your correct first name, last name, phone number, and email address. The rest of the data record should be made up. Because of the design of the database, you may only choose a City value that is in the drop-down list.

24. You should notice and/or test the following items covered throughout this exercise:

    • What is the Caption of the Email field?

    Email Address

    • Can you enter 15000 in the salary field? What happens when you do?

    No, a message keeps popping up asking to enter a salary above $20,000

    • Is the City drop-down list working properly? What values appear in the list?

    Yes, the values are Amherst, Buffalo, and Clarence

    • What happens when you type **Rochester** into the City field for your record?

    A message pops up asking to select one from the list

- Can you leave the City field blank?

  _No_

- How does your phone number appear in the database table?

  With a parenthesis mark around the area code and a dash after the first three number following (315) 385-1584

- What happens when you attempt to edit the data in the Full Name field?

  Nothing because the field is read-only.

- What is the default value appearing in the State field for new records?

  _NY_

- What is your EmployeeID in the database table?

  _18_

- How does your Hire Date appear in the database table?

  For example: 9/11/2013

25. If you plan to continue with the Chapter 2 Applied Exercise, keep this database open. Otherwise, you can close the database and save it for future use.

Chapter 2 Applied Exercise

This is your first Applied Exercise, so it is important for you to understand that this is designed to test your knowledge of what you have learned so far and to **expand your knowledge** a little beyond what is explicitly covered in this textbook. You will often find the F1 key to be helpful in accomplishing what needs to be done.

Prior to working on this Applied Exercise, you must complete the Chapter 2 Guided Exercise. Once you have completed the Guided Exercise, continue using the **Employees.accdb** database for this Exercise. Do *not* download a new version of the database from the course website. You need to continue using the same file you have been working on already.

1. Add a field named Evaluation to the Employees table and use the Lookup Wizard data type to create a drop-down list of the following values: Excellent, Very Good, Good, Average, Below Average, Poor.

2. Using the drop-down list you just created, assign sample Evaluation data for every data record in the Employees table.

3. Create a new table named Titles; it should contain the fields TitleCode and TitleName. Both fields should be assigned Text data types. Enter the following three records of data. To create a new table, select Create ribbon and click the Table icon.

TitleCode	TitleName
MGR	Manager
REP	Sales Representative
EX	Executive

4. Assign appropriate Captions and Field Sizes for the two fields. Assign TitleCode as the primary key.

5. Add a field named TitleCode to the Employees table and use the Lookup Wizard data type to create a drop-down list based on the values in the Titles table. Do *not* select the option "I will type in the values that I want." The drop-down list should display *both* the TitleCode and TitleName in the drop-down list. To do this, **make sure you uncheck the option for Hide Key Column** as shown in the following screenshot.

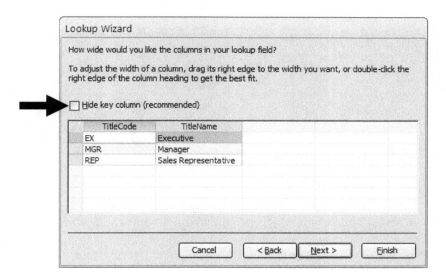

6. Adjust the properties of the TitleCode field in the Employees table so that the end user can enter *only* data items from the drop-down list.

7. Using the drop-down list you just created, assign TitleCodes for each record in the Employees table.

8. Add a Validation Rule and appropriate Validation Text to the HireDate field in the Employees table. This rule should allow only hire dates on or before today's date. Hint: Part of the solution is to use the **Date()** function in the Validation Rule. **Date()** will always return the current date.

9. Change your HireDate to today's date.

10. Add a field named Resume to the Employees table that can store your resume in the table. Do *not* use the OLE Object data type.

11. Add your resume to the database table in your record.

12. Add a field named Employee Code to the Employees table. Assign this field as a Text data type.

13. Create a custom Input Mask for the Employee Code field that requires the entry of three letters, then a dash, then three numbers (e.g., ABC-123). The input mask should also display all of the letters in uppercase. Hint: Use F1 to search the Input Mask help as suggested in the previous Guided Exercise.

14. Add sample Employee Code data for each record in the table.

Throughout the Chapter 2 Guided and Applied Exercises, you have had the opportunity to work with tables in the Datasheet and Design View. Chapter 3 will build upon this chapter and explain how forms are used to simplify the entry of data into database tables. Before continuing, make sure you are comfortable building tables and are familiar with how data types and field properties prevent GIGO in a database.

Simplify Data Entry with Forms

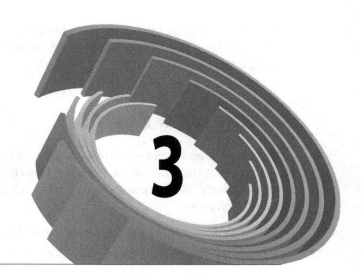

3

Introduction

So far in this textbook, you have learned what databases are and how they can generate information to support decision making. In the previous chapter, you learned how tables should be designed and built in an Access database to prevent GIGO (garbage in, garbage out). If you have not completed the Guided and Applied Exercises in Chapter 2, it is strongly recommended that you do so before continuing in order to familiarize yourself with the use of databases in decision making and the specifics of designing and building database tables.

This chapter begins a detailed look at the next database object: **forms.** Here is the description of database forms provided in Chapter 1.

- "Forms are based on tables or queries, and they are used for entering data into the database in a user-friendly manner. They are also used for displaying data to the end user and can be used to create a menu system for the database."

Now that the foundation (tables) of your database has been established, you can continue building your database upon this foundation. One common need for most databases is to create a way to facilitate data entry in a user-friendly fashion. To address this need, this chapter will explain the ways forms are used in databases, the major types of forms, and the technical specifics of designing and building forms in Microsoft Access.

What Can You Do with Forms?

Forms are mainly used for three things: editing data, viewing data, and creating a menu system. The menu system will be covered in Chapter 7, so this chapter will focus on how we use forms to facilitate entering data and viewing database data. Without forms, you would have to enter data directly into tables, which is usually more difficult.

Forms used for entering data and viewing data are built directly from tables or queries and provide a custom way to view, interact, edit, add, and delete the data in real time. It is important to understand that there is a direct "connection" between the form data and the table data. Any change you make to data on the form is actually modifying the table data at the same time. Refer back to the Chapter 1 Guided Exercise (step 10) for a refresher of what a basic form looks like and how it can be used to enter and display data from a table.

Designing Forms

Because the end users of your database will likely use forms to do most of their work in the database, it is important that they be well designed. Well-designed forms are more efficient and often less frustrating to work with. Here are some basic user interface design principles to keep in mind when designing and building forms.

- Forms should have a consistent look and feel.
- Text on forms should be easy to read.
- Forms should be pleasant to look at and easy on the eyes.
- Functionally, forms should display all relevant information in a logical fashion.
- Forms should employ intuitive and consistent navigation.
- The layout and design of forms should reflect the way the end user works with the form data.

To save time when building forms, I recommend that you first make your form functional, and then make it look nice. In other words, the primary challenge is to make sure it works! Once the form is working properly, you can make necessary adjustments to the design. I suggest method this because you can waste a lot of time tweaking and retweaking the form design while you are building it.

While considering how the end user will be working with the data, you also have to decide what type of form to create. In a Microsoft Access database, you can choose to build a combination of **Basic Forms, Multiple Item Forms, Split Forms,** or **Subforms.** Subforms are covered as a separate topic in Chapter 6, so this chapter will focus on the other types of forms. Basic Forms, Multiple Item Forms, and Split Forms are fundamentally the same to work with and build, except they allow you to interact with the table data in different ways.

- **Basic Forms** display one record of data on a form at a time.
- **Multiple Item Forms** display multiple records of data at the same time. These are also referred to as Continuous Forms.
- **Split Forms** are like a combination of a Basic Form and a Multiple Item Form all wrapped into one big form. On a Split Form, you can view a single record in its entirety and also view multiple detailed records of data at the same time. Split Forms are so named because you can view and interact with the data in two ways simultaneously.

Building and Working with Forms

Microsoft Access has numerous wizards that aid you in the creation of database objects. I strongly recommend that you use the **Form Wizard** to help you when creating a new form. The Form Wizard provides a great framework that you can customize and build upon, which saves a lot of time. Often, the Form Wizard can build approximately 70% of the form for you instead of you having to build every single piece of the form "from scratch." Specific details of working with the Form Wizard will be covered in the Guided Exercise of this chapter.

Once the form is created, it can be viewed in the **Form View, Layout View,** or the **Design View.** Each view has its distinct purpose, advantages, and disadvantages, which are summarized here. While building database forms, you will often switch between these views.

- **Form View** is the end-user view of the form used for entering and displaying data. You can fully update and work with the form data in this view, but you cannot make any changes to the form design or layout.

- **Design View** provides the most powerful way to work in the design and layout of the form. In this view, you cannot see or work with any of the form data.

- **Layout View** is a combination of Form View and Design View. It enables you to make most design changes to the form while viewing live form data, but you cannot update the data you are viewing. It is very powerful because it instantly allows you to see how design changes will look on the form with data.

Before diving into the details of building a form in the Guided Exercise, it is important to be familiar with a little more terminology related to forms and to understand the principle of inheritance when building a form.

First, anything you see on a form is called a **control.** This includes items such as labels, textboxes, combo boxes, option groups, checkboxes, images, command buttons, and even graphical lines. We will explore each of those items in detail in the Guided Exercise, but for now, it's important that you understand that we generically can refer to any of those items as a control. Controls can be further classified as Bound, Unbound, or Calculated:

- A **bound control** is bound or "connected" to a specific field in an underlying table or query. When the data in a bound control is updated, it is ultimately updating the field in the table from which the form is built. Textboxes, combo boxes, option groups, and checkboxes are some common controls that are usually bound to an underlying data source.

- An **unbound control** is not connected to any underlying data source in a table or query. Images, labels, and other graphics are common examples.

- A **calculated control** is based on a formula, function, or expression that displays a calculated result. Although calculated controls often use underlying data fields as part of the calculation, they are unable to update any data in the table like a bound control can. As the underlying fields used in the calculation are updated, the result displayed in the calculated control is also updated. The results of calculated controls are usually displayed in textboxes on a form.

When you build a form or add controls to a form, those controls will inherit the properties of the table fields. This is referred to as **inheritance.** It is a pretty simple concept, but it can get tricky when you start making changes to your tables after forms are already built.

If the field properties in the table are modified *after* the form is built, in some cases the form controls will not inherit the changes! For example, if a database has an existing form built from a table and you decide to make one of the fields in the table a combo box using the Lookup Wizard, the form will *not* automatically display that field on the form as a combo box. To ensure that control has inherited the most recent field properties from the table, you should **delete the control on the form and then add it to the form again.** At the time the control is added, it will inherit the field properties from the table (including the combo box) and will display automatically as a combo box on the form.

Chapter 3 Guided Exercise

1. Download the **Customers.accdb** file from the course website. After you click on the filename on the website, you will have to select either the "Save" or "Save to Disk" option depending on the web browser you are using. **Do NOT choose the Open option.** You should save the file to your desktop, flash drive, or other convenient location.

2. After downloading the file, navigate to where it is stored on your computer. Double-click the **Customers.accdb** file to open it in Microsoft Access 2010.

3. Click the **Enable Content** button on the Security Warning notification that appears.

4. Click on the drop-down list above the Navigation Pane to ensure you have both the **Object Type** and **All Access Objects** options selected to display. This is illustrated with a screenshot in the Chapter 1 Guided Exercise if you need help with this step.

5. Double-click the **Customers** table to open it in Datasheet View and add a sample record for your Teaching Assistant in the table. You can do this by entering the data below the last record. Use the correct first and last name of your TA. The rest of the data record for your TA should be made up. Close the table after you have added the record.

6. Double-click the **Products** form to open it in Form View. Click the **Next Record** command button on the form to browse through a few records of data on the form.

    Based on the data stored in the table, what types of products does this company sell?

    Technology / Computer / Networking

7. Click on the **Product Name** control to select it and then click the **Find Record** command button to find the record for the **3' Network Patch Cable.** You may have to adjust the search options on the **Find and Replace** window that appears in order to find that record.

    What is the ProductID for this record?

    Product ID: 3

8. Click the **Add Record** command button on the form to add the following record.

    Product Name: Laser Printer

    Units On Hand: 150

    Product Description: Black and white laser printer. 15 ppm output.

    Product Image: Double-click the control to add the **printer.jpg** file available from the course website.

    Date Introduced: 8/7/1999

    Eligible for Discount: Yes (Check the checkbox.)

    Product Category: Hardware

    Manufacturing Plant: Buffalo, NY

    Cost: $55.00

    Selling Price: $135.00

9. As mentioned earlier in the chapter, everything you see on the form is called a control. On this form, the words "Product ID," "Product Name," and "Units on Hand" are stored in **unbound**

controls called **labels.** Labels are used to display static text on the form; that is, the text does not change.

The Product ID, Product Name, and Units on Hand **data** are stored on the form in a **bound control** called a **textbox.** These are probably the most common bound controls used to display data.

In addition, there is a **checkbox** control used for the Eligible for Discount data, and there is a **combo box control,** which stores the Manufacturing Plant data. Fields with Yes/No data types in the table will automatically appear as checkbox controls on a form, and fields that have been configured as combo boxes (drop-down lists) in the table will automatically appear as combo boxes on the form.

One other type of control worth pointing out is the **command button** control. The buttons you see on the bottom of the form, called command buttons, can perform various actions. Other types of controls can be used on a form, but these are the common types you will most often use and see.

10. Select the **Home** ribbon and click on the **View** button drop-down menu in the upper left-hand corner to switch to the Layout View of the form. Notice that in this view, you cannot add or edit the data in the form. As mentioned earlier in this chapter, this is an example of one of the limitations of the Layout View when working with forms.

    Right-click on the **Product ID** control and select **Properties** from the context menu that appears. Click on various controls on the form. Notice that the **Property Sheet** displays the properties for the control you have selected. These properties can be adjusted to change many settings on the form. As you select a few controls, briefly examine the different properties for each one.

11. Switch the drop-down menu on the Property Sheet to display **Form.** This will show the general properties for the entire form.

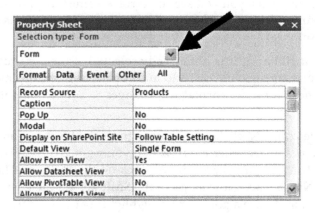

One very important property for the form is the **Record Source.** This property shows which table or query the form is built from. When you click on the **Record Source** property, you will see that a drop-down list appears where you can switch it to another table or query.

What is the Record Source property for your form?

Products

Important Note: If the form was built using the Form Wizard, it is possible that the Record Source uses a special embedded query that is stored within the form. If the Record Source does not show a table or query name but instead displays something like this, **SELECT [Customers]. [CustomerID],** you know that the form was built using the Form Wizard. The code you would see is actually a query, which can be edited if necessary. To modify the embedded query, click on the **Record Source** property to select it and then click the **Build** button (⬚) that appears next to the Record Source row.

12. With the Property Sheet displayed and Form still selected in the drop-down list, click on the **Format Tab** of the **Property Sheet** and look for the **Default View** property. This property determines whether the form will display as a Basic (Single) Form, Multiple Item (Continuous) Form, or Split Form. These three types of forms were described earlier in this chapter.

    What is the Default View property for this form?

    _____ Single Form _____

13. Click on the **Units on Hand textbox** (not the words "Units on Hand," but the control next to it, which displays the actual data) to select it. The Property Sheet should now be displaying the properties for that control. Click on the **All** tab of the **Property Sheet** and look for the **Control Source** property.

    What is the Control Source property for the Units on Hand textbox?

    _____ Units on Hand _____

    This property is telling you the field or expression the textbox is referencing in the underlying table or query. In other words, this is where it is getting its data from. It is **very important** to be familiar with this property when trying to fix errors on your form.

    Often, people will rename fields in their tables or queries, leaving some form controls "orphaned," meaning they are now pointing to (referencing) something that no longer exists. When this happens, you will see the error **#Name?** display in the textbox on the form. When you encounter this error, check this property to see why it is not referencing a valid field or expression.

14. Select the **Format** ribbon if it is not already selected. Take a minute to look through the different font, formatting, controls, and autoformatting options available on this ribbon. You can apply these font and formatting changes to single controls or multiple controls simultaneously.

    To select multiple controls, click on a control, press the **Shift** key on the keyboard, and then continue selecting as many other controls that you want. To try this, click on the **Product ID** label, press the **Shift** key on your keyboard, click on the **Units on Hand** label, and lastly, click on the **Product Name** label. Now let go of the **Shift** key on the keyboard. All three labels should be selected and have a gold border highlighting each control. Next, change the font to the font of your choice. You should see all three labels switch to that font because they are all selected.

    To undo this font change, press **Ctrl + Z** on your keyboard. This is a handy keyboard shortcut for Undo in all Microsoft Office programs. If you keep pressing **Ctrl + Z**, it will keep undoing what has been done.

    Ctrl + Y will **redo** something if you accidentally undid it. Press **Ctrl + Y** now and you should see the three controls switch back to the font you previously selected. Press **Ctrl + Z** once more to switch the controls back to the original font.

15. You can also resize individual controls or multiple controls simultaneously. In the Layout View, many forms are designed to allow you to resize all of the controls simultaneously. For example, click on the **Product Name textbox** to select it. Now place your mouse pointer over the far right side of the textbox, directly over the highlighted outline of the textbox. When you do this, your mouse pointer turns into a double arrow. When you see that, you can drag the border of the text-box to expand or shrink its size. Doing so will also adjust the size of all the textboxes on the form.

    Adjusting the size of an individual textbox may be a bit more involved in Layout View. First, press **Ctrl + A** on your keyboard to select all of the controls on the form. Next, right-click on any of the highlighted controls, select **Layout** from the context menu that appears, and click on **Remove Layout** option from the submenu that appears. Now, click on the **Units on Hand textbox** to select it, and resize it smaller. This time, only the selected textbox will be resized.

    You can still resize multiple controls simultaneously. To do so, use the **Shift** key to select multiple controls. You can then resize one of them, which will resize all of them the same way.

16. A useful feature in Microsoft Access is **Conditional Formatting.** Let's try an example that highlights products for which the Units on Hand value is less than 100 units. First, click on the **Units on Hand textbox** (not the words "Units on Hand", but the control next to it, which displays the actual data). Next, select the **Format** ribbon and click the **Conditional Formatting** button on the toolbar. Click the **New Rule** button. Set a condition where the **Field Value Is less than 100.** Below the condition, adjust the format so that the font will appear white and the background will appear red. Click **OK** twice and browse through the records to see if the conditional format is working properly.

17. Select the Design ribbon and click on the **Add Existing Fields** button on the toolbar. This will display the field list, which shows all the data fields you can add from the underlying Record Source. These are all the fields from the table or query used as the form Record Source. If you need to add a field that is not in the list, you will have to either modify the query the form is based on or create a new query to replace the existing Record Source.

    Look in the field list for the **WarrantyLength** field. Drag it from the field list and drop it below the Selling Price control on the form. It should now automatically appear on your form below Selling Price. If it does not appear there, you can drag the new WarrantyLength textbox and label to that location. The Layout View makes it easy to move controls around on the form.

    Double-click the **WarrantyLength** label to edit it and add a space between the words "Warranty" and "Length." The label should now appear as **Warranty Length.** You can double-click on any label to rename it. Update the title at the top of the form, which currently reads **Products,** to display your full name.

18. Click the **Date and Time** button on the toolbar and click **OK** to add the current date and time to the form. It should appear in the upper right-hand corner of the form. Next, select the **Format** ribbon and click the date to select it. On the toolbar, you will see a drop-down list in the Formatting section. Click on the drop-down list to switch the date format to **Medium Date.**

    In the same fashion, switch the current time to display in the **Medium Time** format. Depending on the data type of the control you have selected, various formatting options will appear in this drop-down list.

    Incidentally, you can also modify the format by opening the Property Sheet for the control and manually editing it there. In fact, most of the adjustments made using the buttons on the toolbar can also be done directly in the Property Sheet if you prefer.

19. Select the **Arrange** ribbon and take a minute to look through the different layout, alignment, and positioning options available.

20. Select the **Home** ribbon and click on the **View** button drop-down menu in the upper left-hand corner to switch to the **Design View** of the form. Notice that you can now no longer see any data on the form. As mentioned earlier in this chapter, this is an example of one of the limitations of the Design View when working with forms.

21. Select the **Design** ribbon if it is not already selected by default and take a minute to look through the additional tools and control options available on the toolbar. Place your mouse over each button to see what they are for.

    You should also note that three parts of the form now display: the Form Header, Detail section, and Form Footer. Anything that is in the Form Header displays at the top of the form, and anything in the Form Footer displays at the bottom of the form. The Detail section is where the actual form data will display and where most of the form controls are placed.

    At the far right is a button used to display or hide the Property Sheet. You can use this button instead of right-clicking on a control and selecting Property Sheet from the context menu that appears.

    Another very important button on this ribbon is the **Tab Order** button. The Tab order of a form is the order in which you move from control to control when pressing the **Tab** key. You want to have this set in a logical fashion so that it is easy for a data entry person to enter data. The Tab order should *not* bounce all over the form. Generally, the Tab order should go from top to bottom and left to right.

    If you have not done so already, click the **Tab Order** button to display the settings. On this window, you can click the button to set an Auto Order or you can manually move the controls up and down in the list. It is a little tricky to move them if you do not know how. First, select **Detail** from the **Section** panel to display the Tab order of the controls in the Detail section of the form. Next, place your mouse next to the word "ProductID." When your mouse hovers over the small box to the left of the word "ProductID," it will turn into a thicker arrow that looks like this: ➡

    Once you see that arrow, you can click your mouse button once to select that control. Once the control is highlighted, you can then drag it up and down the list to reset the Tab order to your liking. Also, holding down the **Shift** key enables you to select adjoining items in the list at the same time.

    For this exercise, set the Tab order from top to bottom and left to right and click **OK** to close the Tab Order window. Depending on the form, it may already be in this order. Click on the **Home** ribbon and click on the **View** button to return to the **Form View** to test the Tab order. Once it is working properly, return to the **Design View** of the form.

22. Click on the **ProductImage textbox** and display the **Property Sheet** for this control. Click on the **Other** tab on the Property Sheet and set the **Tab Stop** property to **No.** Switch back to the Form View and press the **Tab** key to test this.

    What happens when you set the Tab Stop property to No for a control?

    When I press the Tab key it skips and does not select ProductImage Textbox.

23. Now, let's add a calculated control that displays the markup amount for each product. To do this, click the **Text Box** button on the toolbar to add a new textbox to the Detail section of the form. The **Text Box** button icon displays the lower case letters **ab**. Click any blank area on the Detail section and an unbound textbox and corresponding label will be added to the form. Next, open the **Property Sheet** of this new unbound textbox and find the **Control Source**

property. Because it is an unbound control, there is no control source entered right now. Enter the following into the Control Source property:

$$= [\textbf{SellingPrice}] - [\textbf{Cost}]$$

Make sure you type this in exactly, or you it will not work properly.

Switch to the Form View to verify that the new calculated control is working properly. Adjust the cost and/or selling price of any product, and the calculated control will immediately and automatically update the result.

Lastly, switch back to Design View and view the Property Sheet once again for the new textbox. Find the **Format** property and switch it to **Currency.** The data will now appear properly formatted in Layout View and Form View. Overwrite the existing data label associated with this control and name it **Markup.**

24. In Design View, you can also set the form as a Single, Continuous or Split form. If you need to, refer back to step 12 to see how to adjust the Default View property of the form. Switch the Default View property to **Continuous** and then click the **View** button to switch to the Form View to see what it looks like. Next, switch the Default View property to **Split Form** and see how it appears in Form View. Lastly, switch the Default View property back to **Single Form.**

25. Adding buttons to a form is very simple. In Design View, make sure the **Design** ribbon is selected. Click on the button named **Button** on the toolbar. If you're having trouble finding it, the Button icon looks like a button with xxxx written on it. Next, click anywhere at the bottom of your form to add a command button and to start the wizard. Once the wizard starts, select **Form Operations** from the **Categories** section and select **Close Form** from the **Actions** section. Click **Next.** Select the **Text radio button** and leave the default **Close Form** text. Click **Next.** Click **Finish.** You should now see a command button with the text "Close Form" on it. Click the **Save** button (picture of a disk), which is directly next to the Access button in the upper-left hand corner.

    Switch to Form View. Click the **Close Form** button to see if it works properly. If you forgot to save your form in the previous step, you will be prompted to save your form at this time. If you are prompted, make sure you select **Yes** to save your form changes.

26. Lastly, we want to switch the Product Category control from a textbox to a combo box. The easiest way to do this is to add the combo box to the table using the Lookup Wizard. We can then replace the existing control on the form with a new one so that it inherits the combo box properties from the table.

    Right-click on the **Products table** and select **Design View** from the context menu that appears to open it. Change the data type for the ProductCategory field from Text to **Lookup Wizard.** Select "**I will type in the values that I want.**" Click **Next.** Enter **Hardware** in the first row. Enter **Software** directly below Hardware. Enter **Networking** directly below Software. Click **Next.** Click **Finish.** Close the table and click **Yes** if prompted to save the changes.

27. Right-click on the **Products form** and select **Design View** from the context menu that appears to open it. Click the **Product Category textbox** to select it and press the **Delete** key on your keyboard to remove it from the form.

    Click the **Add Existing Fields** button on the toolbar to display the field list. Drag and drop the **ProductCategory** field onto the form. Switch to **Layout View** and resize the textbox as necessary. Switch to the Form View to ensure that the combo box is working properly. Close the Products Form and click **Yes** if prompted to save the changes.

28. So far in this exercise, we have worked with a form that was already built. Briefly, let's see how to build a form using the Form Wizard and the canned form formats available.

   Click once on the **Products table** to select it. Click the **Create** ribbon. Click the button named **Form** on the toolbar. This will automatically create a form based on the table or query you have selected. Close the form and do not save the changes. The **Split Form** and **Multiple Items** form buttons work the same way and can be found by clicking on the **More Forms** button on the toolbar. Try those two options as well, but save only the Multiple Items form you create. Save the form with the name **Products Multiple.**

   Lastly, click the **Form Wizard** button on the toolbar to start the wizard. The first step of the wizard asks where you want to get the data for your form. If it is not already selected, choose **Table: Products** in the drop-down list. Below that, you have the option to pick some or all of the fields from that table. Click the **double arrow** to add all of the fields. Click **Next.** Click **Next.** When asked, "What title do you want for your form?" enter the name **ProductsWizard.** Click **Finish.** As you can see, the form wizard is an easy and powerful way to create a large portion of your form automatically.

29. If you plan to continue with the Chapter 3 Applied Exercise, keep this database open. Otherwise, you can close the database and save it for future use.

Chapter 3 Applied Exercise

Prior to working on this Applied Exercise, you must complete the Chapter 3 Guided Exercise. Once you have completed the Guided Exercise, continue using the **Customers.accdb** database file for this Exercise. Do *not* download a new version of the database from the course website. You need to continue using the same file you have been working on already.

1. Open the Customers Form and add yourself as a customer.

2. Open the Customers Form in Design View and adjust the underlying Record Source property to access the Customers Query instead of the Customers Table.

3. Change the Default View property of the form from Split Form to Single Form.

4. Fix any controls that are no longer referencing valid fields by updating their Control Source property to reference a corresponding field in the Customers Query.

5. Add the CustomerType, Discount, and TotalPurchases fields to the form.

6. Add a calculated control that multiplies Discount and TotalPurchases. Modify the control so that it displays the results in a Currency format. The label for this control should be named Total Discount.

7. Add a Conditional Formatting Data Bar for the Total Discount control. Hint: Select the "Compare to other records" rule type to create a Data Bar.

8. Add a calculated control to display the current date in the Form Footer. Adjust the control to display the date using the Long Date format.

9. Remove the Fname and Lname controls. Add the Name control to the form from the Customers Query to replace these.

10. Change the CustomerType control to a combo box. The combo box should contain the following customer types: Educator, Senior, Student, Veteran, Corporate, and Other.

11. Add Command buttons to add a record, delete a record, find a record, and close the form.

12. Add a label to the Form Header that contains your full name.

13. Add a graphic or logo of your choosing to the Form Header.

14. Put the finishing touches on the form and save it.

- Resize textboxes so that all field data displays.

- Update the default textbox labels. For example, use **Loyalty Club** instead of **LoyaltyClub.**

- Align all controls neatly.

- Reset the Tab order.

Throughout the Chapter 3 Guided and Applied Exercises, you have had the opportunity to design and build various forms. You will find that most of what you have learned in this chapter also applies to building reports, which is covered in Chapter 5. Fortunately, there is a lot of overlap of material when working with forms and reports in Microsoft Access.

Before working on reports in Chapter 5, we will explore the topic of queries in Chapter 4. Although the Chapter 4 exercises do not build directly upon the material covered in this chapter, it is very important to understand the material covered previously in Chapters 1 and 2 before continuing.

Obtain Valuable Information Using Queries

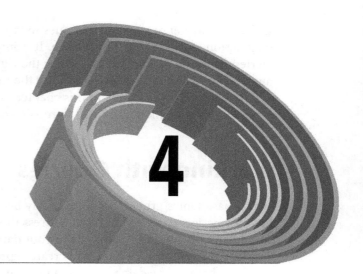

4

Introduction

As mentioned in Chapter 2, databases are well suited for providing information that supports decision making. Often, the process to turn database data into information requires a **query** to be built in Microsoft Access. Here is the description of database queries provided in Chapter 1.

- "Queries enable you to extract data from your database tables and allow us to answer questions we have about the data. Queries may combine data from multiple tables and manipulate data output through the use of expressions, formulas, and functions."

Not only will this chapter teach you the nuts and bolts about queries, but it will hopefully expand your thinking about what questions could potentially be asked of a database. Knowing the "right" questions to ask of your database in a business environment is just as important as knowing how to build that question into a database query.

What Can You Ask of a Database?

When working with databases in a business, it is up to you to know the "right" questions to ask your database. Assume you are managing a retail store with numerous sales employees working on sales commission. Here are some basic examples of questions you may ask your retail store database.

- Which are the best-selling products?
- Which employees are the most productive?
- What day and time of week is busiest in your store?
- What products have the highest profit margin?
- What are the total dollar sales by product each day this week?
- What is the price for a particular product?
- What products in inventory have never sold?

As the store owner or manager, the questions you could ask are potentially endless and limited only by your imagination and need for information. It is important to realize that vast amounts of information may be queried from the database if you know the right questions to ask—and you know how to formulate that question into a database query. Knowing the right questions to ask comes with managerial experience and will not be covered as a topic in this chapter. Instead, this chapter will explain how to translate a question or request for information into a Microsoft Access query.

Working with Queries

As database tables grow in size, it quickly becomes difficult to scan through the data records to retrieve the information you want. We can address this difficulty in building queries designed to extract and view **limited** amounts of information from your database tables. In addition to limiting the data results, you can sort the results, group the data, and create expressions (calculations) based on existing data in the tables. If you think back to the database design guidelines discussed in Chapter 2, you will recall that one guideline is to avoid storing calculated or derived data in a table. We will see in this chapter how queries are used to create those calculations as needed.

Any query can be saved and rerun at a later time. Each time a query is run, it will retrieve the most recent data from the database tables to generate the output. As a result, queries are often used as the basis for database forms and reports.

It is also important to understand that there is a direct "connection" between the query output and the table data. Any change you make to data in the query output is actually modifying the table data at the same time. This is similar to the connection we saw earlier between forms and tables.

The number and types of data records returned in the query output can be limited by setting **criteria** in a query. Much of the Guided Exercise in this chapter will explain the technical details of setting different types of criteria in a query. In addition to the basic AND and OR criteria, other functions such as Like, In, Between, Null, and Parameters will be covered. In addition, you will learn how to create a **Grouped** or **Totals** query.

There are six main types of queries that can be built in Microsoft Access.

- **Select** displays specific fields and data records from a table or tables based on the criteria set. This is the most common type of query and is the focus of the Guided Exercise in this chapter.

- **Make Table** creates a new table and populates it with the results of the query.

- **Append** adds (appends) the results of the query to an existing database table.

- **Update** updates various fields and records in a table based on the criteria set.

- **Crosstab** creates an interactive crosstab output based on the criteria set.

- **Delete** deletes specific records in a table based on the criteria set.

This book focuses on Select queries and touches very briefly on other action queries (Make Table, Append, Update, and Delete). Also, because we are still working with simple databases, the examples in this chapter are usually based on a single table database instead of a multiple table relational database. Fortunately, almost everything covered about Select queries in this book also applies to action queries and multiple table queries, so the knowledge you learn is easily transferrable when you need to develop a more advanced query.

Building Select Queries

Although Microsoft Access has the **Simple Query Wizard** to help build Select queries, I do not recommend using it because you really need to understand how a query is built and works. Instead, you should create a new query in the Design View, which allows you to work with the nuts and bolts of the query design.

There are three exceptions to my advice about using wizards for building queries in Microsoft Access. The **Crosstab Query Wizard, Find Duplicates Query Wizard,** and the **Find Unmatched Query Wizard** help you easily build these specific types of advanced queries. Although these types of queries are not commonly built, I suggest that you use their respective wizards when you need to build those queries.

Once you have a query created, you can view it in the **Datasheet View, SQL View,** or the **Design View.** While building and testing database queries, you will mostly switch between the Datasheet View and Design View.

- **Datasheet View** is the end-user view that displays the results of the query after it is run. Any changes and updates made to the data in the Datasheet View will update the table automatically.

- **Design View** is the view used to build and design queries. Using this view, you can set criteria, select specific fields to output, and sort the data, among other things. In this view, you cannot work directly with any of the query data.

- **SQL View** is an advanced view that allows you to edit the SQL (structured query language) code for the query. SQL is not covered in this book, but it is a powerful way to create queries using a command line interface. As you make changes to the query in the Design View, it will automatically update the SQL code in the SQL View, and vice versa.

Chapter 4 Guided Exercise

1. Download the **StudentRegistration.accdb** file from the course website. After you click on the filename on the website, you will have to select either the "Save" or "Save to Disk" option depending on the web browser you are using. **Do NOT choose the Open option.** You should save the file to your desktop, flash drive, or other convenient location.

2. After downloading the file, navigate to where it is stored on your computer. Double-click the **StudentRegistration.accdb** file to open it in Microsoft Access 2010.

3. Click the **Enable Content** button on the Security Warning notification that appears.

4. Click on the drop-down list above the Navigation Pane to ensure you have both the **Object Type** and **All Access Objects** options selected to display. This is illustrated with a screenshot in the Chapter 1 Guided Exercise if you need help with this step.

5. Double-click the **Students** table to open it in Datasheet View and add a sample record for your Teaching Assistant in the table. You can do this by entering the data below the last record. Use the correct first name, last name, and email address of your TA. The rest of the data record for your TA should be made up. Close the table after you have added the record.

6. Select the **Create** ribbon and click on the **Query Design** button to begin creating a new query. The first thing to do is decide what this query will be built from. Double-click the **Students** table in the **Show Table** windows that appears. This should add the Students table to the Design View behind the **Show Table** window. This table will appear as a list of all the fields in the Student table. Click the **Close** button.

What you are seeing now is the Design View of a query. At the bottom of the window is an area called the QBE (query by example) grid. Only the fields added to the grid will appear in the query output.

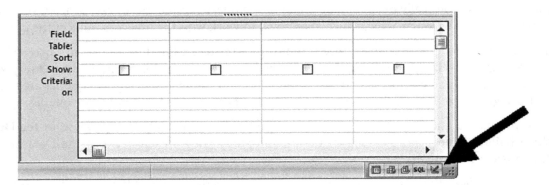

At the bottom right-hand corner are shortcut buttons you can use to switch between the SQL, Design, and Datasheet Views of a query. There are also buttons to switch to the Pivot Table and Pivot Chart Views, but those are not covered in this book. If you place your mouse pointer over the button, a Tooltip appears, indicating which view it corresponds to. In the preceding screenshot, the Design View button is selected.

The rows of the QBE grid are somewhat self-explanatory. The **Field** row indicates which field is selected, and the **Table** row indicates which table that field is from. The **Sort** row enables you to sort data in ascending or descending order. If you sort on multiple fields, the sort precedence is from left to right. In other words, it will first sort the data on a leftmost sort field; the query will then sort additional fields within that sort order.

The **Show** checkbox enables you to show or hide the particular field output. This is useful when you want to search or sort on data but you do not want the end user to see those data that may potentially be sensitive.

The **Criteria** rows are used to limit the data that are returned. The word **or** below Criteria indicates that **OR criteria** appear on separate rows in the QBE grid. This will be explained in much greater detail later in this exercise.

7. There are a few different ways to add fields to the QBE grid to include them in the query output.

   a. First, double-click on the **Student Name** field in the Students table that appears in the Design View of the query. When you do this, it should add the Student Name field to the QBE grid.

   b. Next, click on the **Field** row in the second column of the QBE grid (which should be blank); a drop-down box should appear. Select **Email** from the drop-down list of available fields. This should add the Email field to the second column of the QBE grid.

   c. Lastly, use your mouse to drag the **Phone Num** field from the Students table to the grid below. You will have to hold your mouse button down while dragging the field.

   d. You can press the **Ctrl** key to select multiple fields at once or the **Shift** key to select multiple adjoining fields in the table. Once they are selected (highlighted), you can drag and drop all of them from the table to the QBE grid at once. Use the **Ctrl** key to select **Force Added** and **Person Num** and then drag them to the QBE grid.

   e. One easy way to add all of the table fields to the QBE grid is to double-click the asterisk (*) in the table. The asterisk will be the first item in the list, and it is a shortcut representation of *all* the fields in the table. Double-click the **asterisk** to add it to the QBE grid.

Your QBE grid should now look something like this:

Field:	Student Name	Email	Phone Num	Force Added	Person Num	Students.*
Table:	Students	Students	Students	Students	Students	Students
Sort:						
Show:	☑	☑	☑	☑	☑	☑
Criteria:						
or:						

8. Moving and deleting fields in the QBE grid is not difficult as long as you know where to position your mouse pointer to select a column. In the previous screenshot, notice the small arrow above the **Force Added** field. The mouse pointer will turn into a small arrow such as that when you position it just above a column in the QBE grid. When the arrow appears, you can the click your mouse to highlight an entire column. Once a column is highlighted, you can then drag and drop it to another location on the QBE grid, or you can delete it by pressing the **Delete** key on your keyboard.

   Delete the **Force Added** column and the **Students.*** column in the QBE grid. Move the **Person Num** column between the Student Name and Email columns. Add the **Class, Major 1,** and **GPA** fields to the QBE grid.

9. Look for the **Run** button, which is next to the **View** button on the Design ribbon. The **Run** button has a red exclamation point icon on the button. The **Run** and **View** buttons both do the same thing and display the query output if you have created a Select query (like our current example), but they operate differently when you are working with an Action query (Make Table, Delete, Append, or Update).

   In an Action query, the **Run** button will perform the action upon the data but will not display any results. In contrast, clicking the **View** button to switch to the Datasheet View will show the results of the Action query but will not perform any action. This is useful if you want to test an Action query to see what results it will create since **you cannot undo an action query once it has been run.** Therefore, once you have adequately tested it, you can then execute the action query using the **Run** button.

   To execute our current query to display the results, click the **Run** button on the Design ribbon. After clicking it, you will be viewing the Datasheet View of the query, which shows all the records from the Students table. In this view, you can add, edit, and delete records just as though you were working directly with the table. Do not make any changes to the data at this time.

10. Click on the **View** button drop-down menu in the upper left-hand corner to switch to the SQL View of the query.

    Delete **Students.Email,** from the SQL code. Make sure you delete the comma after the word "Email" and do not delete any more or any less.

    What is now the SQL code for the query?

    [Student Name], Students.[Person Num], Students.[Phone Num], Students.Class, Students.[Major 1], Students.GPA

11. Click on the **View** button drop-down menu in the upper left-hand corner to switch to the Design View of the query.

How did editing the SQL code in the previous step affect the Design View of the query?

Editing the SQL code also change in Design View of the query

What fields appear in the QBE grid?

Student Name, Person Num, Phone Num, Class, Major 1, GPA

12. Next, click on the **Sort** row in the **GPA** column and select **Descending** from the drop-down list that appears. Also, uncheck the **Show** checkbox in the **GPA** column to hide that in the query output. Run the query again. You should see the students listed in GPA order from highest to lowest.

13. Switch back to the Design View of the query and look for the **Return drop-down list** on the Design ribbon. By default, the drop-down list will have **All** selected. Click on the drop-down list and switch this to **5.** Run the query again, and you will now see the top five best-performing students.

14. Close and save this query by clicking on the LOWER X in the upper right-hand corner of the database. Clicking on the UPPER X will close the entire database instead of just the query. When prompted to save the query, click **Yes** and save it with the name **Top 5 Students.** You will now see this query listed in the Navigation Pane on the left-hand side of the window. Each time the query is run, it will retrieve the most recent table data. Therefore, the query results may change as the GPA records of students change over time.

15. Select the **Create** ribbon and click on the **Query Design** button to begin creating a new query. Double-click the **Students** table in the **Show Table** windows that appears. Click the **Close** button.

16. Add the **Student Name, Person Num, Phone Num, Class, Major 1,** and **GPA** fields to the QBE grid.

17. Run the query and examine the data in the Class field.

What are the unique two character Class codes you see in the output?

_FR, SO, SR, JR_

18. Switch back to the Design View of the query. In the Criteria row of the Class column, enter the code **jr** and then press the **Enter** key to move the cursor to another row.

What did Access automatically do to the criterion that you added?

automatically put quotation mark around the code jr

Depending on the field data type, Microsoft Access will do different things to the criteria you add. For example, criteria for Number fields will not change at all, but criteria for Date/Time fields will be enclosed with number signs (#). Also, Microsoft Access is not case sensitive. This means you can enter lowercase **jr** for the criterion even if the data are stored as uppercase **JR.** Other database software programs are case sensitive, so be careful if you are using a different database application in the future.

19. Run the query and examine the output. You will notice that the query now returns only records where the Class field matches the code JR that you entered. This is the most basic example of using a single criterion in a query to limit the output.

20. Switch back to the Design View of the query. We now want to modify the query so that it displays records from the Students table where the Class field matches JR or SR. This is an example of an **OR criteria,** which was briefly mentioned in step 6 of this exercise. In other words, as the query is executed and "looks" through the Students table, it will display all records with Class field of JR or SR.

    To build this, add the criterion **SR** to the row below the current **jr** criterion. Whenever criteria appear on separate rows in the QBE grid, this represents an OR criteria. Run the query and examine the output. You will notice that the query now returns records where the Class field matches the JR or SR.

21. Switch back to the Design View of the query. We now want to modify the query so that it displays records from the Students table where the Class field matches JR or SR and the GPA field is greater than or equal to 3.5. The addition of the GPA criterion is an example of an **AND criteria.** In other words, as the query is executed and looks through the Students table, it will display any record if the Class field matches JR or SR and the GPA also is greater than or equal to 3.5.

    To build this, add the criteria >=**3.5** to the first criteria row under the **GPA** column. Because we already have an OR criteria established for Class, you have to add the >=**3.5** criteria again to the second row under the **GPA** column. See the screenshot that follows.

Class	Major 1	GPA
Students	Students	Students
☑	☑	☑
"jr"		>=3.5
"SR"		>=3.5

Criteria on the *same* row, like "jr" and >=3.5, are interpreted as **AND criteria** by Microsoft Access. In other words, both conditions must be met for a record to be returned in the query output.

This is how to "read" the query you have just created: the query will return all records from the Students table where the Class is equal to JR and the GPA is greater than or equal to 3.5 or where the Class is equal to SR and the GPA is greater than or equal to 3.5. Run the query and examine the output to see the data that are returned.

How many records are returned in the query output?

6

22. Switch back to the Design View of the query. This query can be simplified a bit, as illustrated in the following screenshot, to return the same output. This approach is a little more intuitive.

Class	Major 1	GPA
Students	Students	Students
☑	☑	☑
"JR" Or "SR"		>=3.5

Run the query and examine the output to see the data that are returned. Verify that the same number of records is returned as recorded in the previous version of the query.

23. Switch back to the Design View of the query. Let's add one more criterion to finalize this query. Add **MG** to the first criteria row in the **Major 1** column. This is how to read the query you have just created: the query will return all records from the Students table where the Class is equal to JR or SR and the Major 1 field is equal to MG and the GPA is greater than or equal to 3.5. In other words, this will display all Junior or Senior level Management students with a GPA greater than or equal to 3.5.

Run the query and examine the output to see the data that are returned. Close and save this query by clicking on the LOWER X in the upper right-hand corner of the database. When prompted to save the query, click **Yes** and save it with the name **Top Performing Management Upperclassmen.**

24. Now that you have learned the basics of AND and OR criteria, you can expand on those as needed to build a variety of queries. Beyond these criteria, there are also advanced functions and criteria that can be used. This next example combines five of these special criteria into one example.

For this example, we will create a query to identify local students who may be eligible for a scholarship. This scholarship is open only to Freshman, Sophomore, and Junior students who are majoring in Management (MG), Management Accounting (MGA), or Computer Science (CSE) with a GPA between 3.5 and 4.0. Only local students are eligible, and the students must not be working toward a second major.

To begin, select the **Create** ribbon and click on the **Query Design** button to begin creating a new query. Double-click the **Students** table in the **Show Table** windows that appears. Click the **Close** button.

25. Add the **Student Name, Phone Num, Class, Major 1, Major 2,** and **GPA** fields to the QBE grid.

26. To identify local students, we will search for students with a Phone Number value that begins with the area code 716. To search for part of a record, you can use the **Like** function in Microsoft Access. Simply enter **716*** (don't forget the asterisk) in the first criteria row under the **Phone Num** column, and Microsoft Access automatically puts in the **Like** function and syntax for you. This will now return any records where the Phone Num field begins with 716 and ends with anything else. The asterisk is a wildcard that can stand for anything. Run the query to test the criteria. Switch back to the Design View of the query.

27. Next, to eliminate Seniors from the results enter <> **SR** in the first criteria row under the **Class** column. The <> notation means "not equal to" in Microsoft Access. Run the query to test the criteria.

28. Now we have to restrict the results to return only Management (MG), Management Accounting (MGA), and Computer Science (CSE) majors. This can be done with an OR command, but we will use this opportunity to show another way to do this using the **IN** function. Enter **In (MG, MGA, CSE)** in the first criteria row under the **Major 1** field. Every item included in the IN function is treated like a separate OR criteria. This is useful when you have numerous items to be included for an OR criteria and is also technically a more efficient way to query a database compared with using multiple OR criteria. Run the query to test the criteria. Switch back to the Design View of the query.

29. Next, we have to ensure that the students do not have a second major. Enter **Null** in the first criteria row under the **Major 2** column. Access will automatically switch this to "Is Null." Null means empty, so if a record is empty, it will be returned in the output when using this particular criteria. This is consistent with what we want the query to do—display students with no second major, which means their Major 2 field should be empty, or Null.

There is a variation of this special criteria that returns the opposite results. The **Is Not Null** criteria will return any records that are not empty. So, if any data exist in a field you set the Is Not Null criteria to, it will return the record in the output. You do not need to use it for this query, but it is worth noting for future reference. Run the query to test the criteria. Switch back to the Design View of the query.

30. Lastly, we want to return only students with a GPA between 3.5 and 4.0. Technically, you could just use the criteria >=3.5, but we'll do something a little different in order to demonstrate the Between function in Microsoft Access. Enter **Between 3.5 and 4** in the first criteria row for the **GPA** column. This will now return only records where the GPA is greater than or equal to 3.5 and less than or equal to 4.

    Run the query to test all of the criteria. If built properly, you are now able to identify the students eligible for the special scholarship. Close and save this query by clicking on the LOWER X in the upper right-hand corner of the database. When prompted to save the query, click **Yes** and save it with the name **Scholarship.**

31. This next example will show you how to build a special type of query called a Grouped or Totals query in Microsoft Access. This type of query allows you to summarize and group data in the query results. Consider an example where you want to display the average GPA for each Major. When attempting to build a Grouped query, it is a good idea to write down or visualize what you want the output to look like. In this case, the output should have each Major listed in a column and the average GPA for all the students in those majors.

    To begin, select the **Create** ribbon and click on the **Query Design** button to begin creating a new query. Double-click the **Students** table in the **Show Table** windows that appears. Click the **Close** button.

32. Add the **Major 1** and **GPA** fields to the QBE grid.

33. Click the **Totals** button on the toolbar. The **Totals** button has the Greek letter Sigma Σ as an icon on it. When you select this, a new row named Totals will be added to the QBE grid. By default, the Totals row will be set to the **Group By** option. This means that the query will create one record for each unique group of data it finds. When you set **Group By** on multiple fields, the query will create one record for each unique combination of records across the output fields.

34. Click on the **Group By** option for the **GPA** column and switch it to **Avg.** The query will now create a single record for each unique Major it finds in the table and will average all of the GPAs within those Major groups. Run the query to see the output. Switch back to the Design View of the query.

35. Change the Totals row in the **GPA** column from **Avg** to **Count.** Run the query to view the output.

    What does the Count function do?

    count the same number of GPA for each major

    Switch back to the Design View of the query.

36. Change the Totals row in the **GPA** column from **Count** to **Min.** Run the query to view the output.

    What does the Min function do?

    show the lowest GPA for each major

    Switch back to the Design View of the query.

37. Change the Totals row in the **GPA** column from **Min** to **Sum.** Run the query to view the output.

What does the Sum function do?

add all the GPA for each major

Switch back to the Design View of the query.

38. Change the Totals row in the **GPA** column from **Sum** to **Max.** Run the query to view the output.

What does the Max function do?

show the highest GPA for each major

Switch back to the Design View of the query.

39. Add the **Class** field before the **Major 1** field in the QBE grid and switch the **Totals** row in the **GPA** column from **Max** to **Avg.** Run the query to see how you can have multiple groups in a query output. This is very useful for quickly summarizing data across multiple dimensions.

Close and save this query by clicking on the LOWER X in the upper right-hand corner of the database. When prompted to save the query, click **Yes** and save it with the name **Average GPA by Major.**

40. This next example will show you how to build a special type of query called a Parameter query in Microsoft Access. This type of query allows you to prompt the person executing the query for criteria as the query is run. This creates an enormous amount of flexibility because the database expert does not have to go into the Design View of the query every time and change the criteria to suit the needs of the end user of the database.

To see an example, double-click the **ClassParameter** query stored in the database to execute it. Enter **JR** when prompted to enter criteria and click **OK.** The query results will now show only students with the Class equal to JR.

Switch back to the Design View of the query. Right-click on the **Criteria row** under the **Class** column and select **Zoom** from the context menu that appears.

Record the criteria you see for the **Class** column below.

[Enter the Class (FR, SO, JR, SR)]

Click **OK** to close the **Zoom** window.

41. As you saw in the previous example, a Parameter query is specified by enclosing the criteria in left and right brackets [ ]. The message that you want the end user to see when the query is run should be enclosed within these brackets. Every time the query is run, the user will be shown the message and prompted for criteria. Whatever the user enters into the prompt will automatically fill in to the corresponding criteria column and row in the QBE grid. It is perfectly OK to combine "hard-coded" criteria on the QBE grid with a single or multiple parameters.

Add the **Major 1** field to the QBE grid and add a parameter for this column containing the message **"Enter a 2 or 3 character Major Code."** To do this, add the criteria [**Enter a 2 or 3 character Major Code**] to the Major 1 column. Run the query and test it with various parameters to see if it is working properly.

Close and save this query by clicking on the LOWER X in the upper right-hand corner of the database. When prompted to save the changes to the ClassParameter query, click **Yes.**

42. This final example demonstrates the use of the powerful **IIF function** and **Data Concatenation** in Microsoft Access queries. For this example, we want to create a query that identifies students graduating with honors according to the following GPA requirements.

> Cum Laude >=3.20
>
> Magna Cum Laude >=3.50
>
> Summa Cum Laude >=3.75

This query should show only graduating students (seniors) who will be graduating with honors (GPA >=3.2). The query should also have an expression using the IIF function that returns Cum laude, Magna cum laude, or Summa cum laude based on the GPA of the student. Lastly, we want to use Data Concatenation to combine the Student Name and Major 1 fields into a single expression that appears formatted like this: **Murray, David (MG)**

To begin, select the **Create** ribbon and click on the **Query Design** button to begin creating a new query. Double-click the **Students** table in the **Show Table** windows that appears. Click the **Close** button.

43. Add the **Student Name, Phone Num, Email, Class, Major 1,** and **GPA** fields to the QBE grid. In the **Criteria** row of the **Class** column, enter **SR**. In the **Criteria** row of the **GPA** column, enter >=**3.2** to restrict the output to seniors graduating with honors. Run the query to test the criteria and view the output. Switch back to the Design View of the query after you have verified it is working properly.

44. Next, click in a **blank Field row** of the QBE grid. Right-click in that blank row and select **Build** from the context menu that appears. This will open the Expression Builder window, which helps you create expressions/calculations of all types in Microsoft Access.

Double-click on **StudentRegistration.accdb** in the left pane that appears in the Expression Builder window. Next double-click on Tables in the submenu that appeared, and then select the Students table. All of the fields from the Students table should now appear in the middle pane of the Expression Builder window. Double-click the **Student Name** field to add it to the Expression Builder. Next, modify the expression to **exactly match** the expression that follows. You will have to manually type in all of the ampersands, parentheses, and quotes in the expression, but the Major 1 field can be included by double-clicking on it like you just did for the Student Name field.

[Students]![Student Name] & " ("& [Students]![Major 1] & ")"

What does this expression mean? The ampersand sign "**&**" is used to concatenate multiple pieces of data into one large expression. In this example, we are connecting the Student Name field with a space and an opening parenthesis, which is then connected to the Major 1 field and lastly connected to a closing parenthesis. All text strings that you want to connect together must be enclosed in double quotes as you see in the preceding example.

Click the **OK** button to close the Expression Builder window.

45. Run the query to make sure the output appears formatted like this: **Murray, David (MG)**

What is the name of the column heading for the new expression you just created?

 Expr1

Switch back to the Design View of the query after you have verified the data concatenation is working properly.

46. Right-click on the **Field** row of the new expression you just created and select **Zoom** from the context menu that appears. Replace **Expr1:** with **MajorName:** to rename the column heading for this expression and click the **OK** button. Run the query and make sure the column heading for the expression is now **MajorName.**

47. The data concatenation should now be working, so let's turn our attention to the **IIF function** used to return an expression displaying the Latin honors each student will receive. Click in a **blank Field row** of the QBE grid. Right-click in that blank row and select **Build** from the context menu that appears. This will open the Expression Builder window, which helps you create the new expression using the IIF function.

    We will first start with a basic example of the IIF function to illustrate how it works; then we will expand on it to create the entire expression. Type the following expression into the Expression Builder window. As we did in the earlier example, you can use the field list to easily add in the correct syntax for the GPA field.

    IIf([Students]![GPA]>=3.75,"Summa Cum Laude","Not high honors")

    What does this expression mean? The IIF function will return one of two outputs depending on what it finds in the GPA field. In this simplified example, if the GPA >=3.75, it will return the text "Summa Cum Laude"; otherwise, it will return the text "Not high honors." Click **OK** to close the Expression Builder window and click the **Run** button to view the query output. Switch back to the Design View of the query after you have verified the IIF function is working properly.

    Our obvious problem is that we want to return one of three possible outputs: Summa Cum Laude, Magna Cum Laude, or Cum Laude. To accomplish this, we have to nest multiple IIF functions inside the other functions. This can get tricky, especially when you are dealing with numerous nested levels of IIF functions. Modify your expression to exactly match the nested IIF expression that follows. Also, add the column heading **Latin Honors** to the new expression.

    IIf([Students]![GPA]>=3.75,"Summa Cum Laude",(IIf([Students]![GPA]>=3.5,"Magna Cum Laude","Cum Laude")))

    The nesting logic allows you to evaluate multiple data inputs and return multiple data outputs as well. The IIF function is extremely powerful and can do many different things.

    Run the query to view the output. Switch back to the Design View of the query after you have verified the IIF function is working properly. Close and save this query by clicking on the LOWER X in the upper right-hand corner of the database. When prompted to save the query, click **Yes** and save it with the name **Latin Honors.**

48. If you plan to continue with the Chapter 5 Guided and Applied Exercises, keep this database open. Otherwise, you can close the database and save it for future use.

Throughout the Chapter 4 Guided Exercise, you have learned to design and build various queries using powerful criteria and functions. If you want additional practice and review with queries, Supplemental Exercises are available in Chapter 9 of this book.

The next chapter builds directly upon this chapter because most reports are built on queries. The Student Registration.accdb file used in the current Guided Exercise will be used and expanded upon in the Chapter 5 exercises, so **make sure you keep a copy of your completed work** for the upcoming chapter.

Create Professional Quality Output with Reports

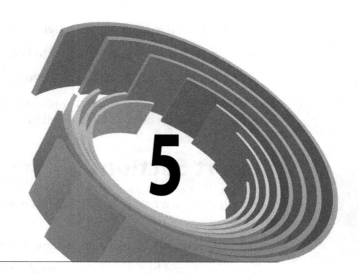

5

Introduction

In the previous chapter, you learned how to create queries that can provide information to support decision making. Often, the query output needs to be presented in a professional format, which requires a **report** be designed and built in Microsoft Access. Here is the description of database reports provided in Chapter 1.

- "Reports use data from a table or query and format the output in a professional-looking manner. Reports provide you with the ability to summarize, sort, group, and display the data in many different ways suited to the needs of the end user. Often, the purpose of a report is to provide a printed output of some data in your database."

If you have not completed the Chapter 4 Guided Exercise, you must do so before continuing, because this chapter picks up where that exercise ended. In addition, the StudentRegistration.accdb database file used in the Chapter 4 Guided Exercise is being expanded upon in this chapter, so it is imperative to complete Chapter 4 before continuing.

Now that you have learned how to extract information from your database using queries, you can format and present this information professionally with reports. Although a large part of building reports simply has to do with the visual presentation of data, there are also simple ways to summarize and group data in a report, which can provide helpful information to the users of your database. In this chapter, we will explore the ways reports are used, the major sections of reports, and the technical specifics of designing and building reports in Microsoft Access.

Lessons Learned from Forms

Almost everything you learned about working with forms in Chapter 3 applies to working with reports! Fortunately, there is a lot of overlap of material when working with forms and reports in Microsoft Access. Here is a basic list of the similarities you will find when working with forms and reports.

- Working with controls (adding, moving, sizing, editing, etc.) and the principle of inheritance are exactly the same in forms and reports.

- Very similar Layout and Design Views exist.

- Visual design principles apply to both forms and reports.

- Property sheet, Record Source property and Control Source property function the same way.

As needed, you may find it helpful to refer back to Chapter 3 to refresh your memory on these topics because they will not be covered in detail this chapter. It is assumed you are familiar with these topics already.

Report Sections

Although there are many similarities when working with forms and reports, there are a few major differences also.

- Reports only display data, whereas forms allow you to display and edit, add, and delete data.

- Command buttons are often used on forms but are rarely used on reports.

- Reports have slightly different design sections compared with forms.

The last bullet point is worth explaining in much greater detail. As you may recall from Chapter 3, forms have a Form Header, a Form Footer, and a Detail section. Anything in the Form Header displays at the top of the form, and anything in the Form Footer displays at the bottom of the form. The Detail section is where the actual form data display and where most of the form controls are placed.

Reports are a bit more sophisticated when it comes to **displaying and grouping** data, so reports contain additional sections that provide this functionality. All reports have Report Header, Page Header, Detail, Page Footer, and Report Footer sections, and special reports that display grouped output will also have Data Header and Data Footer sections. In addition, a grouped report will have a separate Group Header and Group Footer for every grouping level of data.

- **Report Header:** Controls in this section will display at the very top of the first page of a report.

- **Page Header:** Controls in this section will display at the very top of every page of a report. They will appear immediately after the Report Header on the first page of the report.

- **Group Header:** This section appears on a report only if you display the report data in a grouped fashion. Every grouping level of data will have a separate Group Header named after the control being grouped. Normally, this section will contain a textbox to display the field you are grouping the report data on. The data result will appear only once for each unique grouping section.

- **Detail section:** The detailed record-by-record data appear in this section of the report. If the report is being grouped, it will display every record within that group and then continue to the Group Footer section.

- **Group Footer:** This optional section appears on a report only if you display the report data in a grouped fashion. Every grouping level of data will have a separate Group Footer named after the control being grouped. Normally, this section will contain a calculated control to summarize the records in the Detail section. Often, records for each group will be counted, averaged, or totaled. After this section is displayed for one unique grouping, the report will return to the Group Header and then display the results for the next data grouping. The iteration over the Group Header, Detail section, and Group Footer continue until every unique data grouping is displayed.

- **Page Footer:** Controls in this section will display at the very bottom of every page of a report.

- **Report Footer:** Controls in this section will display on the last page of a report immediately after the last Detail section records and Group Footer results are displayed.

Here is an example to further explain how the different sections of a report are used to display data differently. The following screenshot shows a portion of the Design View of a grouped report from the StudentRegistration.accdb database. This grouped report is grouped by the Class field. In other words, this report will display each unique class (Freshman, Sophomore, Junior, Senior), and then a list of students in that class group. An explanation of the output displayed from each report section follows.

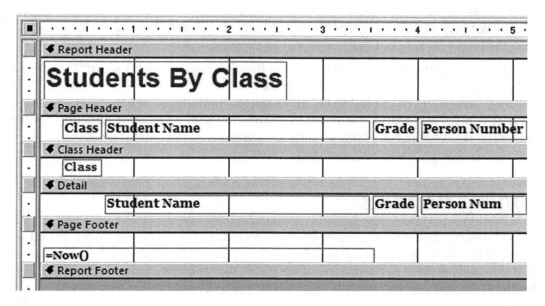

- **Report Header:** This section will display the words "Students By Class" at the very top of the *first* page of the report.

- **Page Header:** This section will display the words "Class," "Student Name," "Grade," and "Person Number" at the top of *every* page of the report. On the first page, they will appear immediately below the Report Header.

- **Class Header:** The Class data will display in a grouped fashion in this section one data grouping at a time. In this example, the unique Class data groupings in the database are Freshmen, Sophomore, Junior, and Senior. Therefore, the output "Freshmen" would appear first, followed by the Detail section listing every freshman student. Once all the freshmen are displayed, the next grouping result, "Sophomore," will appear, followed by the Detail section listing every sophomore student. This iteration through the Class Header and Detail section will continue until all of the data groupings are displayed.

- **Detail section:** As mentioned in the previous section, the Student Name, Grade, and Person Number data will display for every student within the current data grouping.

- **Class Footer:** There is none in this example! Remember, this section is optional even when grouping data. If the section did exist, it might contain a calculated control that displays the total number of students in each data grouping. In other words, it will show the total number of freshmen, the total number of sophomores, and so on. The calculated control =**Count(*)** added to this section will do just this.

- **Page Footer:** The calculated control =**Now()** is used to display the current date and time. This will appear on the bottom of *every* page of the report. The Report Wizard will automatically add this calculated control to the Page Footer of a report you create.

- **Report Footer:** Although you can see the Report Footer bar in this example, there is actually no Report Footer section in this example because the section has been shrunk down to a height of 0. This can easily be expanded by dragging the bottom of the Report Footer bar down to resize that section.

  If the section was being used, it might contain a calculated control that displays the total number of students on the entire report. This result would display after the very last Detail section record on the last page of the report. The calculated control =**Count(*)** added to this section will do just this.

If you have been paying attention, you will notice that the same expression, =**Count(*)**, can be used in both the Class Footer and Report Footer sections. Although the exact same expression is used, it will result in different display outputs. This demonstrates a very important principle when working with reports: **where you put a data control in a report will result in different display outputs or possibly different results!** For this reason, it is very important that you fully understand how the different sections of a report render the data, especially when working with grouped reports.

Designing Reports

Well-designed reports should be organized, grouped, sorted, and presented in a manner that is useful for the **end user** of the database. If you are building reports that other people will be using or viewing, it is critical that you involve them in the process of designing the report to ensure that it meets their needs. It is very helpful if the end user can provide you with an existing paper report that matches the format and design of the report you are building. If a report does not exist, you should work closely with the end user to develop a hand-written mockup of how the report should look. This will then become the basis for your design of the Microsoft Access report.

Once you have a paper design of the report, the next task is to figure out what table or tables your report data come from. If you need to display data from multiple tables in your report, you will first need to build a query, or if using the Report Wizard, Microsoft Access will build the query for you. That table or query is then assigned to the Record Source property of the report (just like forms).

The following was mentioned in Chapter 3 already, but it also applies to reports and is worth mentioning again. To save time, I recommended that you first work to make your report functional, and then make it look nice. In other words, the primary challenge is to make sure it displays the data properly! Once the report is working properly, you can make necessary adjustments to the design. I suggest this because you can waste a lot of time tweaking and retweaking the report design while you are building it.

Building and Working with Reports

I strongly recommend that you use the **Report Wizard** to help you when creating a new report. The Report Wizard provides a great framework that you can then customize and build upon. Often, the Report Wizard can build about 70% of the report for you instead of you building every single piece of the report from scratch. Specific details about working with the Report Wizard will be covered in the Guided Exercise of this chapter.

In addition to the Report Wizard, there is also a separate **Label Wizard** that is used for creating and printing mailing labels. There are hundreds of canned label formats stored in Microsoft Access, and you can also create custom label sizes if necessary. In the wizard, you can easily filter the label sizes by manufacturer, and then select the product number of your blank mailing labels. The Label Wizard will do the rest to ensure that the label spacing and printing works properly for your labels.

Once you have a report created, you can view it in the **Report View, Design View, Layout View,** or **Print Preview** mode. Each view has its distinct purpose, advantages, and disadvantages that are summarized here. While building database reports, you will often switch between these views.

- **Report View** is used for viewing all of the report data, but it does not show page breaks. You cannot make any design changes in the Report View, but you can apply and remove data filters and instantly see how the output updates.

- **Design View** provides the most powerful way to work on the design and layout of the report. In this view, you cannot see any of the report data.

- **Layout View** is a combination of Report View and Design View, which is new to Access 2007. It enables you to make most design changes to the report while viewing live report data. It is very powerful because it instantly allows you to see how design changes will appear on the report with data. In this view you cannot edit the form data.

- **Print Preview** enables you to see all of the report data and pagination exactly how it will appear when the report is printed. You cannot make any design changes to the report in Print Preview.

Chapter 5 Guided Exercise

Prior to working on the following Guided Exercise and Applied Exercise, you must complete the Chapter 4 Guided Exercise. After you have completed the Chapter 4 Guided Exercise, continue using the same **StudentRegistration.accdb** database for these Exercises. Do **NOT** download a new version of the database from the course website. You need to continue using the same file you have been working on already.

It is also strongly recommended that you complete the Chapter 3 Guided and Applied Exercises if you have not done so already. The exercises in this chapter are written assuming you are familiar with the topics covered in Chapter 3.

1. Find the **StudentRegistration.accdb** file you worked on for the Chapter 4 Guided Exercise and navigate to where it is stored on your computer. Double-click the **StudentRegistration.accdb** file to open it in Microsoft Access 2010.

2. If necessary, click the **Enable Content** button on the Security Warning notification that appears.

3. Click on the drop-down list above the Navigation Pane to ensure you have both the **Object Type** and **All Access Objects** options selected to display. This is illustrated with a screenshot in the Chapter 1 Guided Exercise if you need help with this step.

4. Double-click the **Students by Class** report to open it in the Report View. You can tell by viewing the output, and often by the report name, that this is a grouped report. This report displays students grouped by Class.

5. Select the **Home** ribbon and click on the **View** button drop-down menu in the upper left-hand corner to switch to the **Print Preview** of the report. You should now be able to view the report as it will appear when printed. Click the **Close Print Preview** button on the toolbar to return to the Report View.

6. Click the **View** button drop-down menu in the upper left-hand corner to switch to the Layout View of the report. At the bottom of the report, the **Group, Sort, and Total** section should appear. If it is not displaying, click the **Group & Sort** button on the toolbar.

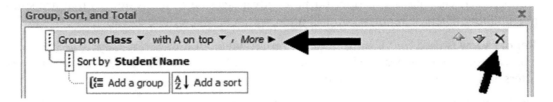

7. The **Group, Sort, and Total** section provides an easy way to see how the data in the report are grouped, sorted, and totaled. In this example, the report is grouped on the Class field, and the detail records are sorted by Student Name within each Class.

8. Click on the triangle next to the word **More** (see arrow on screenshot) to display all of the grouping options. Change the option "**with A on top**" to "**with Z on top.**"

   What happens to the report data when you switch this option?

   the class and student name fields sort from
   _Z - A_

9. Click the drop-down list for the "**by entire value**" option and switch it to the "**by first character**" option. Click your mouse pointer anywhere on the report to apply this change.

   What happens to the SO and SR data groups when you switch this option?

   nothing happen

   Press **Ctrl + Z** on your keyboard to undo the change you just made.

10. Click the drop-down list for the "**with no totals**" option and switch the **Total On** option to the **Student Name.** Check the box for **Show Grand Total** and check the box for **Show Subtotal in Group Footer.**

    List each group and the total number of students in each group:

    _SR = 5, SO = 4, JR = 4, GR = 0, FR = 5_

11. Click on the word "Class" in the "**with title Class**" option. In the pop-up box that appears, change the word from **Class** to **Undergraduate Class.** Click the **OK** button. You will now see the column heading changed from Class to Undergraduate Class.

12. Click the words "**Sort by Student Name**" in the **Group, Sort, and Total** section to select it. Click the **Delete** button (✖) on the far right of this section (see arrow on previous screenshot) to delete this sorting option. You will notice the Student data are no longer sorted in the report.

13. Click the **Add a group** button in the **Group, Sort, and Total** section. Select **Major 1** from the list that appears to add a secondary grouping level on this field. You should now see the data grouped by Major 1 within each Class.

14. Click on the words "**Group on Undergraduate Class (Class)**" in the **Group, Sort, and Total** section to select it. Click the **Move Down** button on the far right of this section. The **Move Down** arrow is next to the **Delete** button you used previously in step 12. Switching this now makes the report group first by **Major 1,** and then groups by **Class** within each Major 1 grouping.

15. Click the **Add a sort** button in the **Group, Sort, and Total** section and select **Student Name** from the list that appears. You should now see the students sorted by name within each grouping level.

16. Click on the Report Title "**Students by Class**" and change it to "**Students by Major and Class.**"

17. Look for the **Themes, Colors, and Fonts** buttons on the toolbar. They are on the far left of the **Design** ribbon. Using these options, you can create customized themes that can be applied to any of the forms or reports you create.

18. Click the **View** button drop-down menu in the upper left-hand corner to switch to the **Print Preview** of the report. On the toolbar, click the **Two Pages** button to display two printed pages on the screen.

    What is on the second page of the report?

    Phone number and email

    _____

19. Click on the **Landscape** button on the toolbar to switch from Portrait to Landscape mode. If you receive an error message stating "**The section width is greater than the page width, and there are no items in the additional space, so some pages may be blank,**" simply click the **OK** button. You should still notice that the second page is blank and has no data even in Landscape mode. Click the **Close Print Preview** button on the toolbar to return to the Layout View.

20. Click the **View** button drop-down menu in the upper left-hand corner to switch to the Design View of the report. Use the scrollbar to scroll to the far right of the report in Design View. Position your mouse pointer on the far right edge of the report; the mouse pointer should change into a two-sided arrow with a vertical line through it (↔). Next, use your mouse to drag the edge of the report to size it to around 9 inches in width. If necessary, resize some of the report controls in Layout View so the report width is no greater than 9 inches.

21. Click the **View** button drop-down menu in the upper left-hand corner to switch to the **Print Preview** of the report. On the toolbar, click the **Two Pages** button to display two printed pages on the screen. Your report should now be at a correct width so that there are no blank report pages. Click the **Close Print Preview** button on the toolbar to return to the Design View.

22. Although this Guided Exercise does not get into the details of working with report controls, remember that much of what was covered in Chapter 3 when working with forms also applies to reports. Adding, moving, resizing, formatting, and deleting controls are done exactly the same way. Also, viewing the properties of specific controls is done the same way.

23. What is the Record Source property for the report? Hint: Check the properties for the entire report the same way you did for the form in Chapter 3.

    _____ _Students_ _____

24. Close and save this report by clicking on the LOWER X in the upper right-hand corner of the database. When prompted to save the report, click **Yes.**

25. Next, let's create a new report using the Report Wizard. Select the **Create** ribbon and click on the **Report Wizard** button to begin creating a new report. The first thing to do is decide which table(s) or query this report will be built from. Click the drop-down list below Tables/Queries and select the query **Latin Honors** from the list.

26. Below that, you have the option to pick some or all of the fields from that query. Double-click the **MajorName, GPA,** and **Latin Honors** fields to add them to the report. Click **Next.**

27. Double-click **Latin Honors** in the list of fields to add it as a grouping level in the report. Click **Next.**

28. Select **MajorName** from the drop-down list to sort the report data on that field. Click the **Summary Options** button. Check the **Avg** box for the **GPA** field and click **OK.** Click **Next.** Click **Next.** Click **Finish.**

29. Click on the **Close Print Preview** button to switch to Design View. Add a label to the Report Footer that says, "**Report prepared by Your Name,**" where **Your Name is your first and last name.**

30. Switch to Layout View. Adjust the column widths so that all the data display properly for each column.

31. Change the **MajorName** column heading to **Student Name.**

32. Delete the **Summary for 'Latin Honors' = Magna Cum Laude (in detail record)** control. Close the report and save it when prompted.

33. If you plan to continue with the Chapter 5 Applied Exercise, keep this database open. Otherwise, you can close the database and save it for future use.

Chapter 5 Applied Exercise

Prior to working on this Applied Exercise, you must complete the Chapter 5 Guided Exercise. After you have completed the Guided Exercise, continue using the **StudentRegistration.accdb** database for this Exercise. Do **NOT** download a new version of the database from the course website. You need to continue using the same file you have been working on already.

Also, this exercise incorporates material from both Chapter 4 and Chapter 5, so you may need to refer back to Chapter 4 to complete this.

1. Create a report based on the Top Performing Management Upperclassmen query you created in Chapter 4. Include Student Name, Person Number, Class, and GPA in the report output. Sort the report output by GPA, with the highest GPA appearing at the beginning of the report. Add conditional formatting so that the GPA will appear in a bold red font if the GPA is greater than or equal to 3.9.

   Format the report properly so that the controls are neatly lined up and all of the report data are displaying. Add a label to the Report Footer that says, "Report prepared by Your Name," where Your Name is your first and last name. Save the report with the name Top Performing Management Upperclassmen.

2. Create a query that includes Student Name, PhoneNum, Class, Major 1, and GPA. Add the following three criteria so that *all* criteria must be met in order for the data output to return.

   - Add a parameter to prompt for Major 1 when the query is executed.

   - Add criteria to further restrict the output to students with a GPA higher than 2.8.

   - Add criteria to display only students with a 716 area code.

In other words, set these criteria so that the query will return only the records for students with a 716 area code who have a GPA higher than 2.8 and have the Major entered in the parameter. All three criteria must be met for the query to return a record in the results.

Save the query with the name Local Students.

3. Create a report based on the Local Students query. Include all of the query fields in the report output. The report should be grouped by Class and sorted by Student Name. In addition, a calculated control should be added to display the average GPA in both the Class Footer and the Report Footer. Format the report properly so that the controls are neatly lined up and all of the report data are displaying. Add a label to the Report Footer that says, "Report prepared by Your Name," where Your Name is your first and last name. Save the report with the name Local Students.

4. Create a new query that includes Student Name, PhoneNum, Class, Major 1, Grade, and GPA. Add the following expressions.

   • Add an expression that concatenates the GPA and Grade so that the output looks like this:

     GPA: 3.7 – Grade: A

     Make sure you also include the text "GPA:" and "Grade:" in the expression. The output should appear exactly as shown here except with different data for GPA and Grade. Name this expression GradeSummary.

   • Add an expression to display Freshman, Sophomore, Junior, or Senior for the corresponding Class codes FR, SO, JR, and SR. Name this expression LongClass. Hint: Use a nested IIF function.

   • Add another expression to display 1, 2, 3, or 4 for the corresponding Class codes FR, SO, JR, and SR. Sort the query on this expression so that the data will display in order of FR, SO, JR, then SR. Name this expression SortClass.

   Save the query with the name Class Sort.

5. Create a report based on the Class Sort query. Include only Student Name, Major 1, LongClass, SortClass, and GradeSummary in the report output. The report should be grouped first by Sort-Class and then by LongClass. The output should be sorted by Student Name. In addition, a calculated control should be added to display the total number of students in each Class and the overall total number of students on the report. The LongClass control should be manually moved into the SortClass Header and the SortClass textbox should be hidden by setting the Visible property to No. The LongClass Header and Footer should be removed from the report so they are no longer displayed. Format the report properly so that the controls are neatly lined up and all of the report data are displaying. Add a label to the Report Footer that says, "Report prepared by Your Name," where Your Name is your first and last name. Save the report with the name Class Sort.

Throughout the Chapter 5 Guided and Applied Exercises, you have had the opportunity to design and build various reports and some queries. I suspect the material may have been very challenging at times, but the good news is that we have now covered the main database objects you will generally work with in a Microsoft Access database. There are two more chapters related to Microsoft Access, but they should be much easier compared with the previous few chapters.

Chapter 6 introduces the topic of relational databases (multiple table databases) along with some of the "fancy" things you can do with multiple tables. Chapter 7 covers a variety of topics, all of which will help you build user-friendly database systems. We are almost finished with the material, so hang in there and keep up the good work!

Design and Implement Powerful Relational Databases

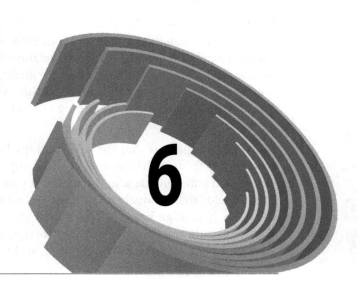

6

Introduction

Microsoft Access is a relational database system, but so far in this textbook, we have not encountered a database that fully leverages the power and features of a relational database system. The point of building and using a database is to utilize its capabilities to handle multiple tables of data. This topic has deliberately been avoided until now because it is much easier to learn the fundamentals of tables, queries, forms, and reports without adding the complexity of dealing with multiple table databases. Now that the introductory topics are covered, it is time to start working with databases as they are truly intended.

This textbook does not explore the complex topic of relational database design; entire textbooks are written on that topic. As a result, this chapter simply focuses on how to implement a relational database in Microsoft Access and assumes that you are working with a properly designed database. All of the examples and exercises in this chapter are based on properly designed databases, but make sure that when you build your own databases, you are familiar with good relational design. In addition, the topic of subforms will be introduced in this chapter.

Why Relational Databases?

Simply put, there are some powerful things you can do with databases that are impossible or infeasible to do with spreadsheets or other applications that store data. Properly designed relational databases are very powerful and flexible and are intended to minimize data redundancy. In addition, once you implement a relational database in Microsoft Access, the software becomes "aware" of how the data are organized and related across the database tables. As a result, the software can then help you build sophisticated queries, reports, and forms built from multiple tables.

Setting Database Relationships

Implementing the relational database in Microsoft Access involves "telling" the database how the fields in one table are related to similar fields in other tables. The "data linking" between the tables that are established are called **relationships.** These relationships must be set properly, because they form the foundation for the database. The database tables are analogous to the bricks of your foundation, and the relationships are the mortar holding the bricks together. Collectively, the tables and relationships form the foundation of your database that everything else is built upon, so you want to make sure you build it properly to begin with!

The rule of thumb is that the relationships between tables should always be between **primary key** and **foreign key** fields with similar data and compatible data types. It is also a good idea to set the relationships before you enter any data in the tables. If you recall from Chapter 2, a primary key is a field or combination of fields that uniquely identifies a record in a table. The primary key can be set in the Design View of the table. A **foreign key** is simply a field in a table that exists as a primary key elsewhere in the database. Oddly, you do not have to "set" the foreign keys in the database tables like you do with primary keys. Foreign keys simply exist by definition, and the database becomes aware of them when you establish the relationship between tables.

The primary key and foreign key fields should also have **compatible data types** in order for the relationship to be set properly. For example, a primary key field with a text data type should relate to a corresponding foreign key field also with a text data type. Generally, if you set the data types of the primary key and foreign key to match, they will be compatible. **There is one important exception to this rule!** Primary key fields with an AutoNumber data type ***must*** relate to foreign key fields with a Number data type. If you incorrectly set both the primary key and foreign key fields to AutoNumber, problems will result once you start trying to enter data into your database. This is a common error, so make sure you pay attention to this exception to the rule.

Once the database primary keys are set properly and compatible data types have been assigned to the primary and foreign keys, you are ready to set the database relationships. There are three additional options you can enable when establishing the database relationships.

- **Referential Integrity:** It is generally a good idea to enforce referential integrity for the relationships in the database. This ensures that foreign key data can be added to a table only if a related primary key already exists. Enforcing this option also prevents "orphaned data" from appearing in your database. Orphaned data are records that exist in the database but are not related to any other data. Because of this, orphaned data are considered "bad" data and should be avoided.

- **Cascade Update:** If referential integrity is enforced, you have the option to also enable Cascade Update for the relationship. It is usually a good idea to enable Cascade Update. This option will automatically update any foreign key values when the primary key field is updated. In other words, it ensures that the data records remain linked together across multiple tables, even if you update the primary key value in the table.

- **Cascade Delete:** If referential integrity is enforced, you have the option to enable Cascade Delete for the relationship. It is not necessarily a good or bad idea to use this option. Instead, you have to decide whether it is something you want for your database system. When enabled, Cascade Delete will automatically delete related foreign key records from the database when you delete a primary key record. If you have multiple tables and relationships with Cascade Delete enabled, it becomes very easy to quickly delete numerous related records from the database. Again, this powerful option should be considered carefully when deciding whether or not to enable it.

The specific details of setting the database relationships and these options will be explained in the Guided Exercise for this chapter.

Using Subforms

Once the database relationships are set, you can take advantage of building **subforms** in your database. Subforms are simply forms inside other forms. The "other" forms the subforms reside in are referred to as **main forms.** The major benefit of subforms is that you can display data from multiple tables on a single form. This allows you to easily present the related data in a logical and user-friendly format.

The most difficult part of building a subform is knowing which table should be used for the main form and which table should be used for the subform. Fortunately, there is an easy rule of thumb you can follow to determine this. To begin, take a look at the relationships you have established in the database. Assuming you have enforced the referential integrity option, the relationship lines should be displaying the type of relationship that exists between each of the tables. Some tables will have the number 1 next to the relationship line, and related tables will have an infinity sign next to the relationship line. The infinity sign represents the term "many," and the relationship is referred to as a one-to-many relationship. If your database is designed and implemented properly, all the relationships in the database should be a one-to-many relationship.

The rule of thumb to follow is that any table on the one side of a relationship can be a main form, and any related table on the many side of the relationship can be a subform inside of that main form. It's that simple.

The specific details of building subforms will be explained in the Guided Exercise for this chapter.

Chapter 6 Guided Exercise

1. Download the **Camp.accdb** file from the course website. After you click on the filename on the website, you will have to select either the "Save" or "Save to Disk" option depending on the web browser you are using. **Do NOT choose the Open option.** You should save the file to your desktop, flash drive, or other convenient location.

2. After downloading the file, navigate to where it is stored on your computer. Double-click the **Camp.accdb** file to open it in Microsoft Access 2010.

3. Click the **Enable Content** button on the Security Warning notification that appears.

4. Click on the drop-down list above the Navigation Pane to ensure you have both the **Object Type** and **All Access Objects** options selected to display. This is illustrated with a screenshot in the Chapter 1 Guided Exercise if you need help with this step.

5. Double-click the **Counselors** table to open it in Datasheet View and add a sample record for your Teaching Assistant in the table. Set the Counselor ID to **15,** set the Location ID to **2,** add the first and last name of your Teaching Assistant, and set the Hire Date to today's date. Close the table after you have added the record for your TA.

6. Open each table in Design View and record the primary key field and its data type below.

    Camper ID - AutoNumber
    Counselor ID - Short Text
    Location ID - AutoNumber

7. Which field is the foreign key field in the Counselors table? What is the data type of that field?

    Location - Number

8. Which field is the foreign key field in the Campers table? What is the data type of that field?

   Counselor ID – Short Text

9. Close all of the tables you have opened. Click on the **Database Tools** ribbon and click the **Relationships** button on the toolbar. This will open the relationships window where we set the database relationships.

10. If a database does not already have relationships set, it will prompt you with the **Show Table** window that appeared. If for some reason the **Show Table** window does not appear, click on the **Show Table** button on the toolbar.

11. Double-click each of the tables (**Campers, Counselors, Locations**) to add them to the relationships window. As you double-click each one, you will see it appear on the screen behind the **Show Table** window. Click the **Close** button after all three tables are added.

12. In each of the tables, you should see the primary key field indicated with a small key icon next to the field. Check to make sure the primary keys match the fields you recorded in step 6.

13. To set the relationship between the Location and Counselors table, click on the **LocationID** primary key in the **Locations** table and drag your mouse over to the **LocationID** field in the **Counselors** table. Make sure you position your mouse pointer directly over the LocationID foreign key field in the Counselors tables before you release your mouse button.

14. The **Edit Relationships** window will now appear. If you set the relationship properly, LocationID should appear twice in the **Edit Relationship** window. Also, the Relationship Type at the bottom of the window should indicate **One-To-Many.**

15. Check the box for **Enforce Referential Integrity** and also check the box for **Cascade Update Related Fields.** Click the **Create** button.

16. To set the relationship between the Campers and Counselors table, click on the **CounselorID** primary key in the **Counselors** table and drag your mouse over to the **CounselorID** field in the **Campers** table. Make sure you position your mouse pointer directly over the CounselorID foreign key field in the Campers tables before you release your mouse button. Check to make sure that the **CounselorID** field appears twice in the **Edit Relationships** window and the Relationship Type is **One-To-Many.**

   Incidentally, it does not matter if you drag the relationship line from the Campers table to the Counselors table or vice versa. Either way, the relationship will appear the same.

17. Check the box for **Enforce Referential Integrity** and also check the box for **Cascade Update Related Fields.** Click the **Create** button. Your relationships window should now look something like this.

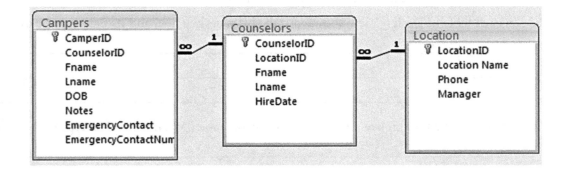

18. Editing or deleting relationships is not difficult but can be a little tricky if you do not know how to do it. To edit the relationship between Counselors and Location, double-click the relationship line that connects the two tables. Once you do this, the **Edit Relationship** window will appear and you can make any necessary changes to it. Click **OK** to close the **Edit Relationship** window.

    To delete a relationship, you must first click on the relationship line to select it. Once it is selected, you can press the **Delete** key on your keyboard to remove the relationship. Try deleting the relationship between Location and Counselors. Click **Yes** when prompted to delete the relationship.

19. Set the relationship between Location and Counselors again making sure to enforce **Referential Integrity** and **Cascade Update.**

20. Click the **Close** button on the toolbar and click **Yes** when prompted to save the changes to the layout of Relationships.

21. Double-click the **Location** table to open it in Datasheet View. Now that the relationships are set, you will see a small plus sign next to each of the records in the table. Click on the plus sign next to LocationID 2 and you will see all the Counselors assigned to that Location. Check to make sure your TA is in the list of Counselors for that Location.

    You will also see a small plus sign next to each of the Counselor records. Click on the plus sign next to your TA's record and add a sample Camper record for yourself. Use your first and last name and set the DOB to today's date. You can make up the rest of the data for your record. After you have added your record, close the Location table.

22. Open the Counselors table and add the following record:

    • CounselorID: 99

    • LocationID: 10

    • Fname: Your first name

    • Lname: Your last name

    • Hire Date: Today's date

23. What is the error message that appears when you attempt to add this record?

    <u>you cannot add or change a record because a related record is required in table 'Location'.</u>

    Why do you think this error appeared? What setting in the database is preventing it from being recorded in the table?

    <u>Because LocationID: 10 is not in the table "Location". Relationships setting is preventing it from being recorded.</u>

    Click the **OK** button to close the error message and change the LocationID from **10** to **1.** Your data record should add to the table properly now. Close the table after the record is modified.

24. Next, your job is to create a subform so that related data from all three tables can be viewed on a single form. Because the relationships are already set in the database, making a subform is very easy. Before making the subform, you need to determine which table will be the main form and which table will be the related subform.

The rule of thumb to follow is that any table on the <u>one side of a relationship can be a main form</u>, and any related table on the many side of the relationship can be a subform inside of that main form. Applying the rule of thumb, what are the two main and subform combinations possible in this database?

Main Form <u>Location</u>

Subform <u>Counselors</u>

Main Form <u>Counselors</u>

Subform <u>Campers</u>

25. The design of this database allows us to create something called a <u>nested subform</u>. This happens when you have a main form that contains a subform. In turn, that subform can also act as a main form and have another subform inside of it, hence a nested subform. In this database, the Locations table is the main form, Counselors is the subform, and Campers is the nested subform inside of the Counselors subform.

26. The easiest way to build these forms and subforms is to let Microsoft Access do it for you! Click the **Location** table once to select it. Next, select the **Create** ribbon and click on the **Form** button. Immediately, you should see a **Locations** main form, with a **Counselor** subform inside of it. As you navigate through the records, you will see that the subform automatically displays only data that are related to the current LocationID displayed.

Click on the plus sign next to any Counselor record and you will then see all of the Campers assigned to that Counselor.

27. Navigate to LocationID 2 and find the Counselor record for your TA. Click the plus sign next to your TA's record and look for your Camper record. Change the **DOB** field to your actual birth date instead of today's date.

28. Close and save this form by clicking on the LOWER X in the upper right-hand corner of the database. When prompted to save the form, click **Yes** and save it with the name **Location.**

29. The next step is to create Linked Forms using the Form Wizard. To do this, select the **Create** ribbon and click on the **Form Wizard** button to start the wizard. The first step of the wizard asks where you want to get the data for your form. If it is not already selected, choose **Table: Location** in the drop-down list. Below that, you have the option to pick some or all of the fields from that table. Click the **double arrow** to add all of the fields. Next, switch the drop-down list of Tables/Queries and select **Table: Counselors.** Click the **double arrow** to add all of the fields from the Counselors table. Click **Next.**

30. Make sure **by Location** is selected and also select the **Linked Forms** radio button. Click **Next.**

31. When asked, **"What title do you want for each linked form?"** enter the name **LinkedLocation** for the first form and **LinkedCounselors** for the second form. Click **Finish.**

32. There appears to be a slight bug in the wizard that puts the command button behind the label for the form title, making it impossible to click! Switch to the Design View of the form and move the label and/or command button so that they are not on top of each other. Switch back to Form View and click the **command button** to see how the Linked Forms work.

33. The final step is to add a Counselors subform and Campers nested subform to the LinkedLocation form we just created. Although it is much easier to have Access create this for you by using the wizards, sometimes you have to add a subform manually.

34. Open the **LinkedLocation** form in Design View. Use your mouse to expand the length of the Detail section of the form.

35. Next, find the **Subform/Subreport** button on the toolbar. This button in the Controls section of the toolbar and is displayed in the following screenshot.

= List box

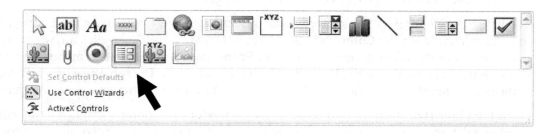

Click the **Subform/Subreport** button once to select it, then click anywhere in the Detail section of the form to start the wizard. Click **Next**.

36. The next step of the wizard asks where you want to get the data for your form. If it is not already selected, choose **Table: Counselors** in the drop-down list. Below that, you have the option to pick some or all of the fields from that table. Click the **double arrow** to add all of the fields. Click **Next**. Click **Next**. Save the subform with the name **Counselors Sub**. Click **Finish**.

37. Next, resize the newly created Counselors Sub subform and expand the Detail section of it. Click the **Subform/Subreport** button on the toolbar, and then click anywhere in the Detail section of the Counselors Sub subform to start the wizard. Refer to the following screenshot to see where to add the new subform. Click **Next**.

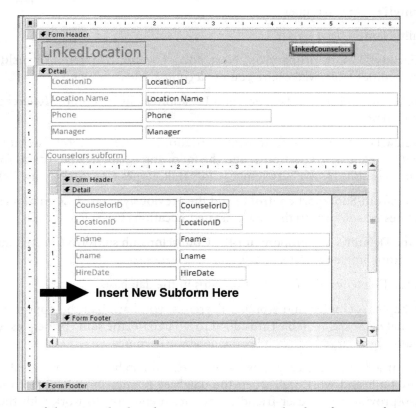

38. The next step of the wizard asks where you want to get the data for your form. If it is not already selected, choose **Table: Campers** in the drop-down list. Below that, you have the option

to pick some or all of the fields from that table. Click the **double arrow** to add all of the fields. Click **Next.** Click **Next.** Save the subform with the name **Campers Sub.** Click **Finish.**

39. You should now have a Locations main form (LinkedLocation), with a Counselors subform (Counselors Sub) and a Campers nested subform (Campers Sub). Close the LinkedLocation form and click **Yes** when prompted to save the changes.

40. To change the Counselors Sub subform from a Datasheet View (looks like a table currently) to a Form View, open the **Counselors Sub** form in Design View. Right-click anywhere on the main form (not the subform) and select **Form Properties** from the context menu that appears. Click on the **Format Tab** of the **Property Sheet** and switch the **Default View** property from **Datasheet** to **Single Form.** Close the form and click **Yes** when prompted to save the changes.

41. Open the **LinkedLocation** form to see how the CounselorsSub subform displays as a form instead of a datasheet. You may need to resize the subform to properly display all of the controls.

42. Close the LinkedLocation form and click **Yes** if prompted to save the form objects.

Chapter 6 Applied Exercise

Prior to working on this Applied Exercise, you must complete the Chapter 6 Guided Exercise. After you have completed the Guided Exercise, continue using the **Camp.accdb** database for this Exercise. Do **NOT** download a new version of the database from the course website. You need to continue using the same file you have been working on already.

1. Create a table named LocationFacilities that contains the following two fields:

   - FacilityID – AutoNumber

   - FacilityName – Text

2. Set the FacilityID as the primary key. Next, add a LocationID foreign key field to the LocationFacilities table. Make sure you use a compatible data type.

3. Set the relationship between Location and LocationFacilities. Enforce Referential Integrity and Cascade Update.

4. Create a new Locations main form with a LocationFacilities subform. Save it with the name Location Complete. For Location 2, add the following FacilityName data as four separate records in the subform: Archery Range, Craft Hall, Ropes Course, Playing Field.

5. Use the Subform/Subreport control to add the previously created Counselors subform and Campers nested subform to the newly created Locations Complete form.

6. Change the Default View property for the CounselorsSub subform (created during the Guided Exercise) from Single Form to Datasheet.

7. Set Cascade Delete for all of the relationships in the database.

Throughout the Chapter 6 Guided and Applied Exercises, you have had the opportunity to explore and work with a relational database. As tables are added to a database, the same principles for setting relationships apply, no matter how large and complex the database becomes.

Also, as you have learned, it is very easy to work with related database data using subforms. Fortunately, subforms are easily built and work well when the database relationships have been set properly in the database. They also provide a very user-friendly way for an end user to work with the database data. In the next chapter, you will learn how to make a database more user-friendly and usable with macros and switchboards.

Build User-Friendly Database Systems

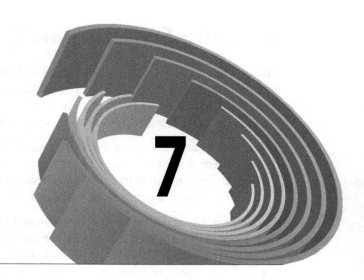

Introduction

After six chapters learning about tables, forms, queries, reports, and relational databases, it is time to combine all of these concepts together into a single, comprehensive, user-friendly database. One way to accomplish this is through the use of macros. Here is the description of macros provided earlier in Chapter 1.

- "Macros are small programs that you build into Microsoft Access; they perform some advanced operations, making the database more user-friendly and/or functional."

Beyond macros, this chapter will also explain how to build a menu system called a **Switchboard** that the end user can use to open various forms and reports in the database. **Navigation Forms,** which are new in Access 2010, will also be briefly introduced as a way to create a user-friendly menu system. In addition, the **AutoLookup** feature will be briefly covered this chapter.

AutoLookup

AutoLookup is a feature in Microsoft Access that makes a data entry form much more sophisticated and powerful to use. It only makes sense to use in certain situations, and based on the design of your database, you might not be able to use it at all. Specifically, the AutoLookup feature can automatically display related data on a form based on the foreign key value you enter. For example, if you enter a Product ID value on a form, AutoLookup will automatically display all of the relevant product information (Product Name, Price, Units on Hand, etc.) on the form.

Generally, you will consider using AutoLookup only when you want a form to display data from two related tables in the database. In this situation, you will first create a query based on those two tables. That query then becomes the basis for the data entry form. The AutoLookup feature is actually a part of the query you build. Because the form is built upon the query, AutoLookup automatically works in the form.

You will have an opportunity to work with the AutoLookup feature in the Guided Exercise for this chapter. It is a difficult concept to explain without working on a live example, so you may want to reread this brief section after you have had a chance to work through the AutoLookup portion of the Guided Exercise.

Building Switchboards

Once you have built user-friendly forms and powerful queries and reports, it is important to give the end user an easy way to work with them. Building a menu system, called a Switchboard, is one way to organize all of the forms and reports logically for the end user. As a result, the end user is also able to avoid the complexity of working with a database system using the Microsoft Access Navigation Pane.

Switchboards are built using the Switchboard Manager wizard, which is accessible from the Database Tools ribbon. There is a limit of eight items per menu page, so if you need additional items, you will need to design a multilevel menu system with multiple menu pages. When the Switchboard Manager wizard is started for the first time in a database, it will check to see if a Switchboard currently exists.

Once a Switchboard is created, a **Switchboard Items table** and a **Switchboard form** will appear in the database. Both of these objects are needed for the Switchboard to work properly, so do not delete them. Another important tip is to make sure you do not delete the command button or textbox on the Switchboard form. If you delete either of them, the Switchboard will not work. The only time you would want to delete the Switchboard Items table and the Switchboard form is if you want to rebuild a Switchboard from scratch.

Switchboard Troubleshooting

Imagine this: you have just spent an hour building a multipage, multilevel menu system and you accidentally delete the Switchboard form. Fortunately, assuming you still have the Switchboard Items table, there is a way to recover much of your work. Each Switchboard button is "stored" in the Switchboard Items table, so we can leverage all of the data in that table to rebuild the form. All we need to do is "trick" Microsoft Access into building another Switchboard form for us. Follow these steps to recover your Switchboard form.

- Rename the Switchboard Items table to **Switchboard Items Old.** Microsoft Access will now think there is no Switchboard in the database because the table has been renamed.

- Start the Switchboard Manager. Click **Yes** when prompted to create a new Switchboard.

- Close the Switchboard Manager and check to see if a new Switchboard form was created.

- Delete the newly created **Switchboard Items table.**

- Rename the **Switchboard Items Old** table to **Switchboard Items.**

- Although you will have lost any formatting changes you made to the Switchboard form, your switchboard buttons are now recovered and should be working!

Alternative Menu Systems

Instead of building a menu system using the Switchboard Manager wizard, you also have the option of creating a custom menu system using a blank form and adding to that form command buttons that open the database forms and reports. The advantages to this approach are that you have much greater design flexibility and you can have an unlimited number of items on the menu, compared with the maximum of eight items on a Switchboard menu. The downside to this approach is that it is not as easy as building a menu system with the Switchboard Manager wizard.

A new way to create a menu system in Access 2010 is with a **Navigation Form.** These special forms have prebuilt templates with horizontal and vertical navigation buttons that are used to quickly access Forms and Reports. Navigation Forms will be briefly introduced in this chapter as an alternative to a Switchboard menu system.

Macros

Macros are small programs you create within the database; they are often used for opening and closing forms and reports. The purpose of macros is to make a database more powerful and easier to use. For example, instead of just opening a form with a command button, a macro could open a form, navigate to a new record on the form, maximize the form window, and place the mouse pointer in a specific form control so that the end user can immediately begin data entry. Although the benefits of this example to the end user might seem miniscule, the advantage in improving your database in small ways with macros become apparent when you consider how many times an end user will perform that same function over a period of a month or a year. The benefits may be small, but they add up over time.

Usually, the macros are associated with a button on a form or switchboard. In other words, the macro is executed when the command button is clicked. There are numerous other ways to trigger the execution of a macro in a Microsoft Access database, but we will focus primarily on macros that are associated with command buttons.

It is impossible to explain every possible thing you can do with a macro, so this chapter will focus on the mechanics of how macros are created and will introduce a few common macro actions. There are dozens of macro actions (commands) you can browse through and research in the Microsoft Access Help to learn what they do and how they work. This chapter focuses on the basic foundation of building macros and executing them with command buttons.

One special type of macro is called an **AutoExec** macro. If you create a macro and save it with the name AutoExec, Microsoft Access will **auto**matically **exec**ute that macro when the database is first opened. Often, the AutoExec macro is used to open the Switchboard form or main menu of the database so that it is the first thing the end user sees when the database is opened.

Other Database Settings

Instead of using an AutoExec macro to open the Switchboard form or main menu, you can set the Current Database startup options to do the same. To modify these settings, click on the **File** ribbon in the upper left-hand corner of Access and click the **Options** button. Next, select the settings for the **Current Database** in the list of categories that appears on the left-hand side of the Access Options window. Look for the **Display Form** drop-down setting and select the form you want to display when the database is opened. The disadvantage to this approach is that you cannot perform any other actions when the database is opened, aside from simply opening a form. In contrast, an AutoExec macro could open a form, maximize the window, and even send a pop-up message to the end user. The options for a macro are endless, whereas the Current Database startup options limit you to simply opening a form.

There are additional Current Database settings that are very useful to set after you have completed your database system. If you want to prevent the end user from accidentally deleting your forms and reports, or if you just want to shield the end user from the complexity of the inner workings of the database, you can hide almost everything except the form that opens when the database starts. To hide these items, uncheck the following items in the Current Database settings: **Display Status Bar, Display Navigation Pane, Allow Full Menus,** and **Allow Default Shortcut Menus.**

The database must be closed and reopened for these options to take effect. You should notice that almost everything is hidden except the form that is set to open when the database starts. But how do you get back into the database to work with the design of the database tables, forms, queries, and reports? To bypass the Current Database startup settings and the AutoExec macro, you need to hold the **Shift** key down on the keyboard while opening up the database. It is advised that you wait to set the Current Database startup options until after your database is fully complete so that you do not have to keep bypassing them every time the database is opened.

Chapter 7 Guided Exercise

1. Download the **Orders.accdb** file from the course website. After you click on the filename on the website, you will have to select either the "Save" or "Save to Disk" option depending on the web browser you are using. **Do NOT choose the Open option.** You should save the file to your desktop, flash drive, or other convenient location.

2. After downloading the file, navigate to where it is stored on your computer. Double-click the **Orders.accdb** file to open it in Microsoft Access 2010.

3. Click the **Enable Content** button on the Security Warning notification that appears.

4. Click on the drop-down list above the Navigation Pane to ensure you have both the **Object Type** and **All Access Objects** options selected to display. This is illustrated with a screenshot in the Chapter 1 Guided Exercise if you need help with this step.

5. Double-click the **Customers** table to open it in Datasheet View and add a sample record for your Teaching Assistant in the table. You can do this by entering the data below the last record. Use the correct first name and last name of your TA. The rest of the data record for your TA should be made up.

   After you have added the record for your TA, click the plus sign next to your TA's record to show the related data in the Orders table. Add an order record for your TA by setting the **OrderDate** to today's date. Close the table after you have added the customer and order record for your TA.

6. Select the **Database Tools** ribbon and click the **Relationships** button to view the database relationships. This database is used to track orders that customers have placed for products. The design you are looking at is the basic design used for most sales orders systems. List each table below and identify the primary key field(s).

   Customers — CustomerID

   Orders — OrderID

   Products - Product ID

   Order Details - OrderID, ProductID

   Click the **Close** button on the toolbar to close the **Relationships** window.

7. The next step is to create an Orders form that incorporates the AutoLookup feature to display data from both the Orders table and the Customers table. As mentioned earlier in this chapter, the AutoLookup feature is actually a part of a query and works only in the form, because the form is built upon the query. So, the first step is to create a query based on the Customers and Orders tables.

   Select the **Create** ribbon and click on the **Query Design** button to begin creating a new query. Double-click the **Customers** table and the **Orders** table in the **Show Table** window that appears. This should add both of those tables to the design view behind the **Show Table** window. Click the **Close** button.

   You should notice that because the Database Relationships are already established, the two tables are automatically joined together by the CustomerID field. When building queries based on multiple tables, it is imperative that the tables be joined properly. Assuming the relationships are correct, the default joins should also be correct.

8. Add all of the fields from the **Orders** table to the QBE grid. Add all of the fields from the **Customers** table to the QBE grid *except* for **CustomerID.** This is extremely important. **For AutoLookup to work, the join field must be taken from the many side of the join and added to the QBE grid.**

Think about that for a second. As you can see in the following screenshot, the join field in this example is CustomerID. We have the option of selecting CustomerID from either the Customers table or the Orders table. For AutoLookup to work, we must select CustomerID from the many side of the join. If you look at the query, you will see that the Orders table is on the many side of the join. Therefore, CustomerID must be taken from Orders and added to the QBE grid.

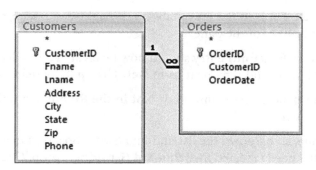

9. To execute the query and display the results, click the **Run** button on the **Design** ribbon. After clicking it, you will be viewing the Datasheet View of the query, which shows all of the related records from the Customers and Orders tables. These results will show one record for every order placed.

Look for the order record you added earlier for your TA and take note of the CustomerID value of your TA. Next, find the record for OrderID **1,** which was placed by customer **David Murray.** Change the CustomerID in that record from CustomerID **1** to the CustomerID of your TA. Once you do that, you should see all of the Customer information for Order 1 switch to display the information for your TA. **That is AutoLookup.**

Switch the CustomerID back to **1** for OrderID **1.**

10. Close and save this query by clicking on the LOWER X in the upper right-hand corner of the database. When prompted to save the query, click **Yes** and save it with the name **CustomerOrders.**

11. Now that AutoLookup is working in the query, we can build a form based on this query. Click once on the **CustomerOrders** query in the Navigation Pane to select it. Select the **Create** ribbon and click the button named **Form** on the toolbar. This will automatically create a form based on the query you have selected. Select the **Home** ribbon and click on the **View** button drop-down menu in the upper left-hand corner to switch to the Form View of the form. Check to make sure AutoLookup is working in the form by adding a **new** record for Customer ID **1.** Set the **OrderDate** to today's date.

On that record, switch the city from **Amherst** to **Buffalo.** As this example demonstrates, even with AutoLookup, you can still update the data in the table.

12. Select the **Home** ribbon and click on the **View** button drop-down menu in the upper left-hand corner to switch to the Design View of the form. Expand the Form Footer section and add a command button to close the form.

Switch back to the Form View and click on the newly created command button to close the form. When prompted, save the form with the name **CustomerOrders.**

13. Now that the Order form is created, the next task is to make a Switchboard menu system that enables the end user to open all of the forms and reports in the database. Currently, this database has three forms and two reports. Since the Switchboard Manager option is hidden in Access 2010, you will first have to add this button to the toolbar in Access. Follow these steps to add this button to the Database Tools ribbon:

- Select the **File** ribbon in the upper left-hand corner of Access and click the **Options** button.

- Select **Customize Ribbon** in the list of categories that appears on the left-hand side of the Access Options window.

- Select **Database Tools** in the list of tabs on the right-hand pane, and click the **New Group** button at the bottom of the pane.

- The **New Group (Custom)** entry should now be created and selected automatically. Click the **Rename** button and rename it from **New Group** to **Switchboard**. Click **OK.**

- Above the left pane, select **Commands Not in the Ribbon** from the **Choose commands from:** drop-down list.

- In the left pane, scroll down the list and find **Switchboard Manager**. Click the **Add** button to add it to the newly created **Switchboard (Custom)** group. Click **OK.**

14. To begin creating the Switchboard, select the **Database Tools** ribbon and click the **Switchboard Manager** button to start the Switchboard Manager wizard. Click **Yes** when prompted to create a Switchboard. If you do not see the Switchboard Manager button, check the previous step to make sure you added it properly.

15. The first page of the Switchboard Manager wizard displays all of the menu pages. To begin, you will have only one menu page, but as the menu grows, you may find it necessary to build a menu system with multiple pages.

    Click the **Edit** button to edit the main Switchboard page. Every item listed on this page represents a separate menu button on the finished Switchboard form.

16. Click the **New** button to add an item to this Switchboard page and set the following options.

    Text: **Open Products Form**

    Command: **Open Form in Edit Mode**

    Form: **Products**

    Click the **OK** button after you have set the options for this button. You may have noticed that there are two similar commands you can use to open forms: Open Form in Edit Mode and Open Form in Add Mode. Open Form in Edit Mode allows you to open a form and view all of the data records that have been previously added. Open Form in Add Mode only allows you to add new records to the database. Unless you want to prevent the end user from viewing and/or changing old records, it is recommended that you use Open Form in Edit Mode when opening forms from the switchboard.

17. Click the **New** button to add an item to this Switchboard page and set the following options.

    Text: **Open Customers Form**

    Command: **Open Form in Edit Mode**

    Form: **Customers**

    Click the **OK** button after you have set the options for this button.

18. Click the **New** button to add an item to this Switchboard page and set the following options.

    Text: **Open Orders Form**

    Command: **Open Form in Edit Mode**

    Form: **CustomerOrders**

Click the **OK** button after you have set the options for this button.

19. Click the **New** button to add an item to this Switchboard page and set the following options.

    Text: **Open Customers Report**

    Command: **Open Report**

    Report: **Customers**

Click the **OK** button after you have set the options for this button.

20. Click the **New** button to add an item to this Switchboard page and set the following options.

    Text: **Open Products Report**

    Command: **Open Report**

    Report: **Products**

Click the **OK** button after you have set the options for this button.

21. Click the **New** button to add an item to this Switchboard page and set the following options.

    Text: **Exit**

    Command: **Exit Application**

Click the **OK** button after you have set the options for this button.

22. You should now have a menu page with five items that looks like this.

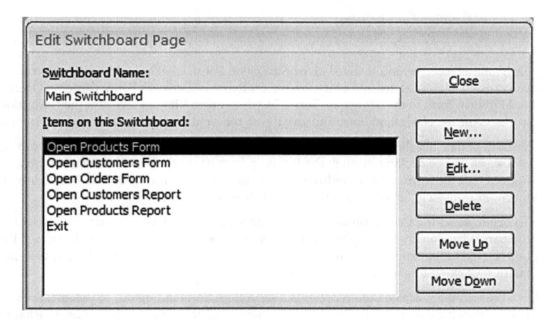

The buttons on the Switchboard form will appear in the same order as the items are listed on this screen. For this menu, rearrange the order so that the Customers and Products reports will appear at the top of the list before the forms. To rearrange the items, use the **Move Up** and **Move Down** buttons. Click the **Close** button twice after you have rearranged the items.

23. You should now have a form in your database named Switchboard. Double-click the **Switchboard** form to open and view it. Try each of the **form** and **report** buttons to see how they work. If you accidentally click the **Exit** button, reopen your database. Close the Switchboard form by clicking on the **Close** button (X) in the upper right-hand corner of the form.

24. Another way to create a similar menu system is by using a Navigation Form. To do this, select the **Create** ribbon, click the **Navigation** button and select **Horizontal Tabs** from the drop-down list that appears. A blank Navigation Form will now appear.

   To add the Products report to the Navigation Form, drag and drop the **Products** report on top of the [**Add New**] button on the Navigation Form. Make sure you drag it on top of the [**Add New**] button so the gold bar appears to the left of the button. This arrow in the following screenshot shows how the vertical gold bar should display just before you drop the report on the form. A common mistake is to drop the report below the [**Add New**] button which causes it to display on every navigation section instead of just the one tab.

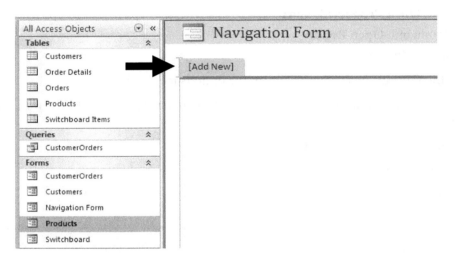

25. Each time a report or form is added to the Navigation Form, another [**Add New**] button appears so you can add additional items. Add the Customers Report, Customers Form, CustomerOrders Form, and Products form to the Navigation Form. Switch to **Form View** and see how the Navigation Form works. Close the Navigation Form and save it with the name **Navigation Form** when prompted.

26. Shifting gears a bit, the next portion of this Guided Exercise will work through a few examples of macros. While clicking through the forms and reports in the previous step, you may have noticed that the forms all have buttons to close the form, but the reports do not. Our first macro example will be to create a button that closes the report.

   To begin, select the **Create** ribbon and click the **Macro** button, which is on the far right of the toolbar. What you are viewing now is the Design View of the macro. You will notice a **Run** button (red exclamation mark) on the toolbar that is the same as the **Run** button used for queries. Clicking this will execute the macro.

   Each row in the macro design represents a separate action (command) to execute. Some macros may have only one action, whereas others may have dozens depending on what you need to accomplish. The actions are executed sequentially from top to bottom.

27. Click on the **Add New Action** drop-down next to the green plus sign and a drop-down list of actions will appear. Take a minute to scroll through the list and briefly browse through the different actions. To create a button to close the reports, select the **CloseWindow** action from the drop-down list.

28. Set the following arguments for the CloseWindow action you just selected.
    Object Type: **Report**
    Object Name: **Customers**
    Save: **Prompt**

29. Close and save this macro by clicking on the LOWER X in the upper right-hand corner of the database. When prompted to save the macro, click **Yes** and save it with the name **CloseCustomers.**

30. Double-click the **Customers** report to open it. Double-click the **CloseCustomers** macro to execute it. The Customers report should close once you double-click the macro.

31. Next, we need to add a button to the report that will be used to execute the macro. To do this, open the **Customers** report in Design View and add a **command button** to the Report Header section of the report. Because reports generally do not use buttons, you will notice that the command button wizard does not start. Instead, you have to manually adjust the command button properties to execute the CloseCustomers macro when the button is clicked.

32. Double-click the command button you just added to open the **Property Sheet** for that button. Select the **Event** tab of the **Property Sheet** and click on the column next to the **On Click** property to display the drop-down list.

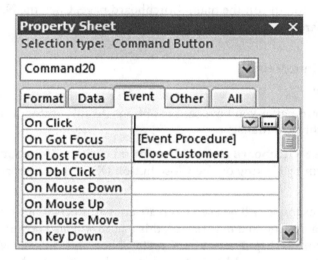

The drop-down list will display all of the macros you have built in your database. In the screenshot, you see the CloseCustomers macro in the list and another option named **[Event Procedure].** The **[Event Procedure]** option is selected if you want to create VBA (Visual Basic for Applications) code to run for this action. VBA is beyond the scope of this textbook, so for our purposes, you can ignore it. Select **CloseCustomers** from the drop-down list. Now, you have assigned the CloseCustomers macro to the command button you created in the previous step.

Edit the command button so that it displays the text "**Close Report**" instead of the default name it was given when it was added to the report.

33. While you are still in the Design View, add a label to the Report Footer that says, "**Report prepared by Your Name,**" where **Your Name is your first and last name.**

34. Switch to the Report View and click the **Close Report** command button to test it. When prompted, click **Yes** to save the report.

35. The next macro example will show you how to create a **Help** button and is intended to demonstrate the **MessageBox** action, which can be used in a macro.

    To begin, select the **Create** ribbon and click the **Macro** button to create a new macro. Click on the **Add New Action** drop-down next to the green plus sign and select **MessageBox** from the drop-down list that appears. Set the following arguments for the MessageBox action you just selected.

    > Message: **Please call 645-3249 for help.**
    >
    > Beep: **Yes**
    >
    > Type: **Information**
    >
    > Title: **HELP!**

36. Click the **Run** button on the toolbar to execute the macro. When prompted to save the macro, click **Yes** and save it with the name **Help.** After the macro is saved, you will immediately see a pop-up message on your screen indicating the phone number to call for help. Click **OK** to close the pop-up message and close the macro.

37. Next, this macro should be added to the Switchboard menu. Select the **Database Tools** ribbon and click the **Switchboard Manager** button on the toolbar.

    Click the **Edit** button to edit the main Switchboard page. Click the **New** button to add a button to this Switchboard page and set the following options.

    > Text: **Help**
    >
    > Command: **Run Macro**
    >
    > Macro: **Help**

    Click the **OK** button after you have set the options for this button. Click the **Close** button twice to exit the Switchboard Manager.

38. Double-click the **Switchboard** form to open it and click the **Help** button to test it. Close the Switchboard form by clicking on the **Close** button (X) in the upper right-hand corner of the form.

39. The final macro example will be used to create an **Add Record** button on the Customers form. In addition to navigating to a new record, this macro will also position the mouse pointer in the Fname textbox. To begin, select the **Create** ribbon and click the **Macro** button to create a new macro. Click on the **Add New Action** drop-down next to the green plus sign and select **GoToRecord** from the drop-down list that appears. Set the following arguments for the GoToRecord action you just selected.

    > Object Type: **Form**
    >
    > Object Name: **Customers**
    >
    > Record: **New**
    >
    > Offset: **[Leave this blank]**

40. Next, click on the **Add New Action** drop-down list immediately below the GoToRecord action you just added. Select **GoToControl** from the drop-down list of actions that appears. Set the following arguments for the GoToControl action you just selected.

    > Control Name: **Fname**

    The macro should now have two actions that will run one after another when the macro is executed. The following screenshot displays what your macro actions should look like.

41. Close and save this macro by clicking on the LOWER X in the upper right-hand corner of the database. When prompted to save the macro, click **Yes** and save it with the name **NewRecord.**

42. Next, we need to add a button to the Customers form that will be used to execute the NewRecord macro. To do this, open the **Customers** form in Design View and add a **command button** to the left of the existing **Close Form** button. Once the wizard starts, select **Miscellaneous** from the **Categories** section and select **Run Macro** from the **Actions** section. Click **Next.** Select the **NewRecord** macro from the list and Click **Next.** Select the **Text radio button** and change the default text from **Run Macro** to **Add Record.** Click **Next.** Click **Finish.** You should now see a command button with the text **Add Record** on it.

    Switch to Form View. Click the **Add Record** button to see if it works properly. If you are now viewing a blank record and the mouse pointer is in the Fname textbox, then the macro worked properly.

43. Close the form and click **Yes** when prompted to save the form changes.

44. If you plan to continue with the Chapter 7 Applied Exercise, keep this database open. Otherwise, you can close the database and save it for future use.

Chapter 7 Applied Exercise

Prior to working on this Applied Exercise, you must complete the Chapter 7 Guided Exercise. After you have completed the Guided Exercise, continue using the **Orders.accdb** database for this Exercise. Do **NOT** download a new version of the database from the course website. You need to continue using the same file you have been working on already.

1. Create a query based on the Order Details and Products tables that incorporates the Auto-Lookup feature. Save it with the name ProductOrders. Next, use this query to add a subform to the CustomerOrders form you created in the Guided Exercise.

    The first two fields in the subform should be ProductID and Quantity and the subform should display the results in the Datasheet Default View. Also, hide the OrderID field in the subform. Hint: Shrink the width of the OrderID control to zero.

2. Using the ProductOrders subform, navigate to the order record for your TA to finish entering the rest of the order in the subform. Add the following two product order records in the subform of your TA's order record.

    - Product ID: 6   Quantity: 2

    - Product ID: 8   Quantity: 1

3. Add a Customer and Order record for yourself. Set the OrderDate to today's date. Add the following two product order records in the subform of your order record.

   - Product ID: 4   Quantity: 2
   - Product ID: 7   Quantity: 1

4. Redesign the Switchboard to include a Main Menu, a Reports Menu, and a Forms Menu. The Main Menu should be modified to display the following four buttons:

   - Open Forms Menu
   - Open Reports Menu
   - Help
   - Exit

   The reports menu should include buttons to open the two reports, and the forms menu should include buttons to open the three forms in the database. Both the reports menu and the forms menu should include buttons that allow the end user to return to the main menu.

   The new Reports Menu should include the following three buttons:
   - Open Customers Report
   - Open Products Report
   - Return to Main Menu

   The new Forms Menu should include the following four buttons:
   - Open Products Form
   - Open Customers Form
   - Open Orders Form
   - Return to Main Menu

5. Add a calculated field named FullName to the Customers table. This field should display both the first and last name with a space between them. Next, modify the Customers report to replace the existing First Name and Last Name fields with the new FullName field. *Hint:* Use the same method for concatenation as explained in Chapter 4.

6. Create a macro that opens the CustomerOrders form, maximizes the form window, navigates to a new record, and positions the mouse pointer in the CustomerID textbox. Save it with the name OpenOrders. Edit the Switchboard so that this macro is used to open the CustomerOrders form.

7. Create a macro that closes the Products report. Save it with the name CloseProducts. Add a command button to the Report Header of the Products report that executes this macro.

8. Create a macro that exits the database. Save it with the name Quit. Edit the Switchboard so that this macro is used to Exit the database. Hint: Look for a macro action that is similar to the name of this macro.

9. Create a macro that automatically opens the Switchboard form when the database is opened and displays a pop-up message welcoming the user to the database. Adjust the Current Database settings to hide the Navigation Pane and menus when the database is opened.

Throughout the Chapter 7 Guided and Applied Exercises, you have learned a few ways to make your database more powerful and user-friendly. Although these seven chapters are by no means comprehensive of all the things you can do with Microsoft Access, they have provided you with a solid foundation upon which to build your knowledge.

Beyond the material covered in this textbook, the next logical topic to learn is VBA. Macros are powerful and can do a lot of things, but the VBA programming language provides even more powerful ways to improve databases. If you are intimidated at the prospect of learning a programming language, I encourage you to consider for a minute all that you have learned in this textbook. Many of you never worked with Microsoft Access before reading this textbook, but look at how much you have learned and accomplished! Although learning a new technology may seem intimidating and overwhelming at times, it is possible to do if you take the time and put your mind to it.

Congratulations on working through all of the Microsoft Access chapters in this textbook!

Team Building and Group Work Exercises

8

Group Icebreaker Exercise

Welcome to your first team task. Over the next few weeks, you will be working in your groups to (1) foster teamwork and team cohesiveness and (2) begin your work on the Project Initial Design. **Good communication** is imperative for any successful team.

The purpose of this activity is to get your team members comfortable working together and to assign group member numbers. Once your TA assigns you in groups, your first task is to assign each member in your group a number from one to five. The member number should be based on the order of your last names alphabetically. Once member numbers have been assigned, each group member should introduce himself or herself and convey the following information. Group member #1 should be the first to start, and this exercise should be done in group member number order.

- Name, email, phone number
- Something unique about yourself
- Birthplace, previous places lived
- Academic background, major, and career aspirations
- Work experience and background
- Hobbies and interests
- What you most want to accomplish in this team

While completing this exercise, **everyone in the group should exchange names, email addresses, phone numbers, and relevant contact information.** There is a convenient place on the inside cover of this lab manual that can be used to record the group contact information. Any absent group members should be contacted by the present group members prior to the next lab.

Your final task to complete as a team in this exercise is to decide on a one-hour standing meeting outside of lab time for the group to meet. It is important to have time set aside for working on your group project outside of the regularly scheduled lab time.

UBLearns Group Collaboration Tools and Team Information Database (TIDB) Exercise

The purpose of this exercise is to get your team comfortable working with each other individually and as a team collectively in an online collaborative environment. Its secondary purposes are to begin the brainstorming process for selecting a project idea and to give you practice using the group collaboration tools on UBLearns and the Team Information Database. Although the project is still a few weeks away, this exercise will help you and your teammates start thinking about what constitutes a good project idea.

The Group Collaboration Tools on UBLearns are very useful for your group while working on the team project and team assignments. They provide a common forum for electronically communicating with your teammates and allow you to collaboratively work on your group assignments with the file exchange. It is strongly encouraged that you utilize these tools as you work on your project throughout the semester. Your TA will provide a brief demo of these tools in lab using a Sample Group comprised of TAs and Professor Murray.

This is your team task to be completed prior to your lab next week.

Group member #1 should download the Team Information Database from the course website, fill out his or her personal information on the Member Form in the database, and post the updated database file on the group file exchange. Before the next lab, each group member should fill out his or her information in the posted database. One caveat is that **this should be done in group member number order,** starting next with group member #2. For example, group member #4 cannot post information until group member #3 has entered his or her data and posted the revised database on the file exchange.

The information entered into the database will be used to generate a report that must be submitted next week in lab and as part of your initial project submission, so be sure to take the time to complete it fully and properly. **One-word descriptions and brief phrases are not acceptable.** Remember that Professor Murray and the TAs will be reading what you enter into the Team Information Database.

The final requirement of this exercise is for group member #4 to print out the final version of the Team Information Report and bring it to lab next week. Your group must communicate with each other to successfully complete this task in the correct order and by the assigned deadline.

Here are some step-by-step directions for working with the Team Information Database. Only group member #1 should download the database file from the course website. All other group members should download the most recent version of the database from the group file exchange on UBLearns and **skip to step #4.**

1. Open the course website in a web browser.

2. Right-click on the Team Information Database link and select "Save Target As" from the context menu that appears.

3. Save the database file on your computer desktop (or any location you prefer).

4. Double-click on the downloaded file to open it in Access.

5. Click the Browse Member Form button on the menu that appears.

6. If necessary, click the Next button to navigate to a blank record. Enter your information and click the Close Form button.

7. Exit Access.

8. Log on to UBLearns, navigate to this course, and click on the Groups button.

9. Click on your group, then click on the File Exchange link.

10. Click the Add File button.

11. Enter an appropriate name for the database (TIDB Member 1 Complete).

12. Click on the **Browse My Computer** button, navigate to the database file saved on your computer, and click **Open.**

13. Click the Submit button to upload the file to your group file exchange.

14. Communicate to the next group member that he or she can fill out his or her information.

Initial Group Peer Evaluation

You now have had an opportunity to complete the UBLearns Group Collaboration Tools and Team Information Database (TIDB) Exercise, which is your first task as a team. How did it go? Were you able to communicate and plan ahead to finish this very easy task, or did you scramble around at the last minute to complete it? Did everyone on your team finish the exercise to the best of his or her ability? It was not intended to be a difficult task, but even so, it may have brought to your attention some of the problems you and your team may be experiencing.

The exercise is intentionally designed and structured so that you have to rely on each other as team members in order to complete it properly. If one member fails to do his or her part, it affects the entire team. If your team experienced this, hopefully it is a lesson you can learn from before you actually start doing the project work.

This peer evaluation is your opportunity to identify the problems in the group (lack of communication, lack of participation, etc.) and to **constructively address** them now rather than later. The peer evaluation form should be completed based on the team performance on the UBLearns Group Collaboration Tools and Team Information Database (TIDB) Exercise.

Please attempt to openly and honestly evaluate the group performance in a way that fosters team growth. Each group should submit a printout of the Members Report from the Team Information Database along with the answers to the following Initial Group Peer Evaluation to the TA.

Database Project Brainstorming Exercise

The purposes of this exercise are to get you and your team members thinking individually and collectively about specific database project ideas and to help you understand what constitutes a good project idea. It is likely that your idea may be used as a basis for your group project later this semester. Upon completion of this exercise, you and each of your group members will have a preliminary idea for the project proposal, which will be submitted to your TA. These ideas will likely need to be refined or completely changed for the actual project proposal, but this exercise will show you how to identify possible ideas that meet the project requirements.

For the project and this exercise, keep these three things in mind. (1) A good project idea is **very important** for your success; therefore, (2) the project must be built for a **real-world** company or organization that you are very familiar with, and (3) your project idea must clearly generate **business value.**

This exercise will walk you through the process of identifying good project ideas that will generate business value. Here is the basic outline of steps to follow.

1. Individually, complete the Database Project Brainstorming Exercise, which begins on the following page. The rest of the exercise builds upon this, so be sure to invest adequate time and thought into your responses to the questions.

2. As a group, share each of your findings from step 1. Based on these findings, begin to brainstorm what might be a good project idea for each group member.

3. Based on your findings from step 1 and the group feedback from step 2, choose your best project ideas and complete the Database Project—Preliminary Project Idea Proposal sheet included in this lab manual. This must be **YOUR idea,** not an idea from another group member.

4. Once everyone has completed step 3, once again share your findings and ideas with your group. Although you may not be able to decide on a final project idea at this time, it is helpful as a group to start thinking along these lines.

5. Submit these proposals to your TA as proof of completion of this exercise.

Database Project—Preliminary Project Idea Proposal

Name _____   Date _____   Lab Day/Time _____

1. What company/organization are you building this database for? Explain how you qualify as a business expert at this place.

   _____

   _____

   _____

   _____

2. Describe the existing system currently in place. If no system currently exists, explain the paper/manual process used.

   _____

   _____

   _____

   _____

3. What business value is the proposed database system is going to create?

   _____

   _____

   _____

   _____

4. In general, what is the proposed database system going to do for the company?

   _____

   _____

   _____

   _____

5. What opportunities is the proposed database system going to take advantage of?

   _____

   _____

   _____

   _____

   _____

6. What problems is the proposed database system going to address? **Be specific.** Do not simply say it will "organize things and save time."

_____

_____

_____

_____

_____

7. What data will be stored in the proposed database system?

_____

_____

_____

_____

_____

8. What information (reports) will be generated by the proposed database system?

_____

_____

_____

_____

_____

Supplemental
Lab Exercises

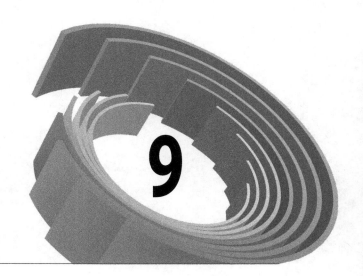

9

LAB EXERCISE #1
Basics of Entity Relationship Diagrams

Name _____ Date _____ Lab Day/Time _____

Use the Entity Relationship Diagram on the following page to answer these questions

1. What is the #1 arrow pointing to called? ___Entity___

2. What is the #2 arrow pointing to called? ___Relationship___

3. What type of relationship exists between Orders and Employees? ___Many-to-One___

4. What is the shorthand notation for a one-to-many relationship? ___1:M___

5. What is the shorthand notation for a many-to-many relationship? ___M:M___

6. What are the two correct questions to ask to determine the relationship between Customers and Orders?
   ___Can one customer has many orders?___

LAB EXERCISE #1
Basics of Entity Relationship Diagrams (cont.)

Name _____ **Date** _____ **Lab Day/Time** _____

7. What are the two correct questions to ask to determine the relationship between Orders and Employees?

_____

_____

8. Place the letter "**P**" next to the primary keys and place the letter "**F**" next to the foreign keys in the entity relationship diagram below.

9. Identify **at least one additional field** for Customers, Orders, and Employees that may be included in the design. Write those fields on the diagram below.

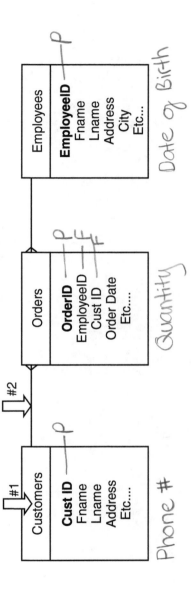

LAB EXERCISE #2
Practice with Entities, Attributes, and Relationships

Name _____ **Date** _____ **Lab Day/Time** _____

Professor Murray has decided to expand the functionality of the Team Information Database so that it can store the team records for **ALL** of the students in the class. Your job as a database designer is to create the database according to the business rules and specifications Professor Murray provides. You should use the Team Information Database as a starting point for the design, but you will also need to add additional entities and attributes. Here are the requirements for the database that you should base your design upon.

- Each lab section has multiple teams.

- Each team has multiple members, but a member can be on only one team.

- Each TA is responsible for multiple lab sections.

In addition to the data already stored in the database, Professor Murray also wants to track the following. Next to each attribute, indicate the appropriate data type to use in Microsoft Access.

- Team Name ___Text___
- TA ___Text___
- Lab Time ___Date / Time___
- Lab Day ___Date / Time___
- Initial Design Grade (score 0–5) ___Numeric___
- Initial Design Comments (usually at least two paragraphs long) ___memo___
- Final Project Grade (score 0–30) ___Numeric___

- Lab Section ___Text___
- Project Website Address ___Hyperlink___
- Lab Location ___Text___
- Project Business Expert ___Yes / No___

LAB EXERCISE #2
Practice with Entities, Attributes, and Relationships (cont.)

Name _____ **Date** _____ **Lab Day/Time** _____

Given the previous requirements, you need to assign the correct entities, attributes, primary keys, foreign keys, and relationships on the blank Entity Relationship Diagram below. In addition, enter the letter **"P"** next to all of the primary keys and place the letter **"F"** next to all of the foreign keys in the diagram.

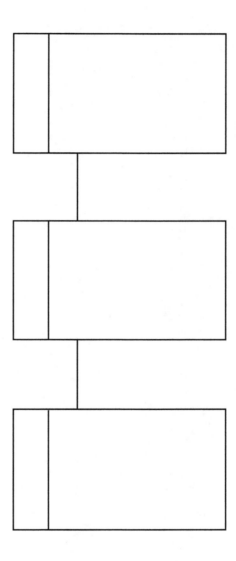

LAB EXERCISE #3
Simplifying Entity Relationship Diagrams (Database Normalization)

Name _____ Date _____ Lab Day/Time _____

1. What is the rule for simplifying one-to-one relationships?

   combine tables no need to have one-to-one relationships

2. What is the rule for simplifying one-to-many relationships?

   properly adding and labeling foreign keys

3. What is the rule for simplifying many-to-many relationships?

   Use intersection table

LAB EXERCISE #3
Simplifying Entity Relationship Diagrams (Database Normalization) (cont.)

Name _____ Date _____ Lab Day/Time _____

4. Draw a simplified version of the entity relationship diagram below the current diagram shown. Make sure you include the appropriate primary and foreign keys. All the relationships should simplify to one to many.

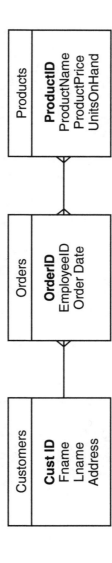

Customers	Orders	Products
Cust ID	**OrderID**	**ProductID**
Fname	EmployeeID	ProductName
Lname	Order Date	ProductPrice
Address		UnitsOnHand

Student Table Datasheet View

Force Added	Student Name	Person Num	Div	Class	Major 1	Grade	GPA
	Murray, David	1234-1234	DUE	SR	MG	A	3.1
	Gilbert, Brendan	1234-5678	DUE	SR	CS	A	3.6
	Baldi, Andrew	1111-1111	DUE	SR	MG	B	3.6
	Anderson, Nate	2222-2222	DUE	JR	MG	B	3.1
	Hill, Kristine	3333-3333	DUE	JR	MG	C	3.4
	Amnott, Scott	4444-4444	DUE	SR	MGA	C	3.8
*	Patil, Smitha	5555-5555	DUE	JR	MG	D	3.7
	Mund, Susan	6666-6666	DUE	JR	MGA	F	3.6
	Kinney, Rachel	7777-7777	DUE	SO	MGA	A	3.1
	Vaz, Ryan	8888-8888	DUE	FR	MG	A	3.9
	Borden, Dave	9999-9999	DUE	SO	MG	R	3.4
	Dinero, Jamie	0000-0000	DUE	JR	MGA	B	3.5

This table is to be used for Lab Exercises 4, 5, and 6.

Student Table Datasheet View (Extra Copy)

Force Added	Student Name	Person Num	Div	Class	Major 1	Grade	GPA
	Murray, David	1234-1234	DUE	SR	MG	A	3.1
	Gilbert, Brendan	1234-5678	DUE	SR	CS	A	3.6
	Baldi, Andrew	1111-1111	DUE	SR	MG	B	3.6
	Anderson, Nate	2222-2222	DUE	JR	MG	B	3.1
	Hill, Kristine	3333-3333	DUE	JR	MG	C	3.4
	Amnott, Scott	4444-4444	DUE	SR	MGA	C	3.8
	Patil, Smitha	5555-5555	DUE	JR	MG	D	3.7
	Mund, Susan	6666-6666	DUE	JR	MGA	F	3.6
	Kinney, Rachel	7777-7777	DUE	SO	MGA	A	3.1
	Vaz, Ryan	8888-8888	DUE	FR	MG	A	3.9
	Borden, Dave	9999-9999	DUE	SO	MG	R	3.4
	Dinero, Jamie	0000-0000	DUE	JR	MGA	B	3.5

This table is to be used for Lab Exercises 4, 5, and 6.

LAB EXERCISE #4
Basics of Queries (Sorting, Showing, Basic Criteria, Grouping)

Name _____ Date _____ Lab Day/Time _____

1. Who is in MGS351 sorted by person number? Include StudentName, Class, and PersonNum fields in the output.

Field:	StudentName	Class	PersonNum			
Table:	Student	Student	Student			
Sort:						
Show:	✓	✓	✓			
Criteria:						
or:						

How many records are returned in this query? ___12___

2. Who are Juniors in MGS351? Include StudentName, Class, and Major1 fields in the output.

Field:	StudentName	Class	Major1			
Table:	Student	Student	Student			
Sort:						
Show:	✓	✓	✓			
Criteria:		"JR"				
or:						

How many records are returned in this query? ___5___

LAB EXERCISE #4
Basics of Queries (Sorting, Showing, Basic Criteria, Grouping) (cont.)

Name _____ Date _____ Lab Day/Time _____

3. Develop a **grouped query** to find out how many Seniors are in this class.

Field:	StudentName	Class
Table:	Student	Student
Total		
Sort:		
Show:	✓	✓
Criteria:		"SR"
or:		

How many records are returned in this query? ___4___

4. Who has resigned from the class? Include StudentName, Class, and Grade fields in the output.

Field:	StudentName	Class	Grade
Table:	Student	Student	Student
Sort:			
Show:	✓	✓	✓
Criteria:			"R"
or:			

How many records are returned in this query? ___1___

LAB EXERCISE #5
Advanced Query Criteria (Null, Like, OR, AND)

Name _____ **Date** _____ **Lab Day/Time** _____

1. Who does not have a grade yet? Include StudentName, Class, and Grade fields in the output.

Field:	StudentName	Class	Grade		
Table:	Student	Student	Student		
Sort:					
Show:	☑	☑	☑		
Criteria:			Is Null		
or:					

How many records are returned in this query? _____ 0 _____

2. Who has a last name beginning with the letter "M"? Include StudentName, Class, and Grade fields in the output.

Field:	StudentName	Class	Grade		
Table:	Student	Student	Student		
Sort:					
Show:	☑	☑	☑		
Criteria:	Like "M*"				
or:					

How many records are returned in this query? _____ 2 _____

LAB EXERCISE #5
Advanced Query Criteria (Null, Like, OR, AND) (cont.)

Name _____ **Date** _____ **Lab Day/Time** _____

3. Who is a Senior OR Accounting major? Include StudentName, Class, and Major 1 fields in the output.

Field:	StudentName	Class	Major 1
Table:	Student	Student	Student
Sort:			
Show:	☑	☑	☑
Criteria:		"SR"	
or:		"MGA"	

How many records are returned in this query? ___4___

4. Who is a Senior AND Accounting major? Include StudentName, Class, and Major 1 fields in the output.

Field:	StudentName	Class	Major 1
Table:	Student	Student	Student
Sort:			
Show:	☑	☑	☑
Criteria:		"SR"	"MGA"
or:			

How many records are returned in this query? _____

LAB EXERCISE #5
Advanced Query Criteria (Null, Like, OR, AND) (cont.)

Name _____ Date _____ Lab Day/Time _____

5. Who is a Junior or Senior and a Mgmt (MG) major? Include StudentName, Class, and Major 1 fields in the output.

Field:			
Table:	Student	Student	Student
Sort:			
Show:	☑	☑	☑
Criteria:			
or:			

How many records are returned in this query? _____

6. Who is a Junior or Senior and a Mgmt (MG) major with a grade of A or B? Include StudentName, Class, Major 1, and Grade fields in the output.

Field:			
Table:	Student	Student	Student
Sort:			
Show:	☑	☑	☑
Criteria:			
or:			

How many records are returned in this query? _____

LAB EXERCISE #6
Advanced Query Criteria (<>, IN, Between, Parameters)

Name _____ Date _____ Lab Day/Time _____

1. Who is not a freshman? Include StudentName, Class, and Major 1 fields in the output.

Field:			
Table:	Student	Student	Student
Sort:			
Show:	☑	☑	☑
Criteria:			
or:			

How many records are returned in this query? _____

2. Who is a freshman, sophomore, or junior? Include StudentName, Class, and Major 1 fields in the output. **Use the IN function.**

Field:			
Table:	Student	Student	Student°
Sort:			
Show:	☑	☑	☑
Criteria:			
or:			

How many records are returned in this query? _____

LAB EXERCISE #6
Advanced Query Criteria (<>, IN, Between, Parameters) (cont.)

Name _____ Date _____ Lab Day/Time _____

3. Who has a GPA between 2.5 and 3.5? Include StudentName, Major1, and GPA fields in the output. **Use the Between func.**

Field:			
Table:	Student	Student	Student
Sort:			
Show:	✓	✓	✓
Criteria:			
or:			

How many records are returned in this query? _____

4. What is the class and major for a specific person number? Include PersonNum, Class, and Major 1 fields in the output. Create a parameter to prompt the user with this message: "Enter a person number."

Field:			
Table:	Student	Student	Student
Sort:			
Show:	✓	✓	✓
Criteria:			
or:			

How many records are returned in this query? _____

LAB EXERCISE #7
Using Subforms Properly

Name _____ Date _____ **Lab Day/Time** _____

Given the following entity relationship diagram, what are two possible ways to create a main form and subform combination?

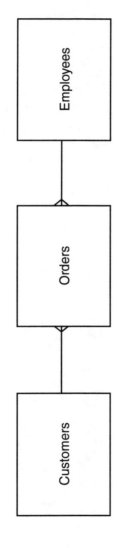

1. Main form _____

   Subform _____

   This would show all of the corresponding _____ records for each _____ record displayed.

2. Main form _____

   Subform _____

   This would show all of the corresponding _____ records for each _____ record displayed.

LAB EXERCISE #8
Using Subforms and Nested Subforms Properly

Name _____ **Date** _____ **Lab Day/Time** _____

Given the following entity relationship diagram, what are the four possible ways to create a main form and subform combination? Write your answers on the following page.

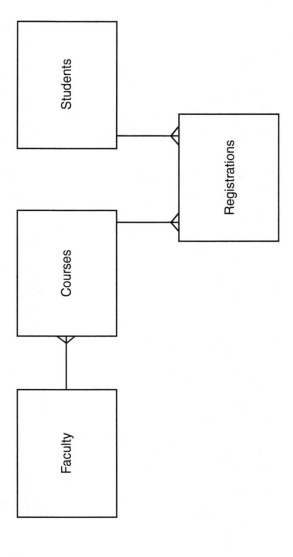

LAB EXERCISE #8
Using Subforms and Nested Subforms Properly (cont.)

Name _____ Date _____ Lab Day/Time _____

1. Main form _____

   Subform _____

   This would show all of the corresponding _____ records for each _____ record displayed.

2. Main form _____

   Subform _____

   This would show all of the corresponding _____ records for each _____ record displayed.

3. Main form _____

   Subform _____

   This would show all of the corresponding _____ records for each _____ record displayed.

4. Main form _____

   Subform _____

   Nested subform _____

   This would show all of the corresponding _____ records for each _____ record displayed and all corresponding _____

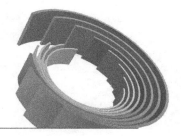

APPENDIX A

HTML Tag Reference and XHTML Compliance

\<br /\>	Line Break
\<hr /\>	Horizontal Rule (line)
\<p\> \</p\>	Paragraph
\<strong\> \</strong\>	Bold
\<em\> \</em\>	Italicize
\<u\> \</u\>	Underline
\<ul\> \</ul\>	Unordered List
\<ol\> \</ol\>	Ordered List
\<li\> \</li\>	Indicates a list item in a list
\&	special character used to display ampersand sign (&)
\®	special character used to display registered trademark symbol (®)
\©	special character used to display copyright symbol (©)
**\ **	special character used to display a blank space
Absolute Link:	**\<a href="http://www.buffalo.edu/~djmurray"\>My Webpage\</a\>**
Relative Link:	**\<a href="index.html"\>My Webpage\</a\>**
Email Link:	**\<a href="mailto:djmurray@buffalo.edu"\>Email to Prof. Murray\</a\>**
Image Tag (Relative):	**\<img src="picture.gif" alt="A Picture" /\>**
Image Tag (Absolute):	**\<img src="http://www.buffalo.edu/pic.gif" alt="A Picture" /\>**

To ensure XHTML Compliance, remember to use lowercase tags and to close **all** tags. Some tags such as \<br /\> are self closing and do not need a separate closing tag. You must also declare the DOCTYPE which is the only tag to be capitalized. Here is the commonly used Transitional XHTML DOCTYPE Declaration:

\<!DOCTYPE html
       PUBLIC "-//W3C//DTD XHTML 1.0 Transitional//EN"
       "http://www.w3.org/TR/xhtml1/DTD/xhtml1-transitional.dtd"\>

XHTML Online Validation Resource http://validator.w3.org

APPENDIX B

Relational Database Design Reference

In an effort to keep the challenging topic of relational database design as simple as possible, the approach taught in this class is somewhat simplified compared with what you will see in other classes and textbooks. In particular, the entity relationship diagram (ERD) notation is simplified, eliminating the often-confusing topics of cardinality and optionality. For your reference, this appendix is a summary of ERD notations, terminology, special ERD considerations, relational database design guidelines, and the relationship simplification rules covered in class. The lecture covering relational database design covers this in much greater detail with examples of these topics.

ERD Notation Examples

There are three types of relationships we can represent on an ERD.

- **One-to-one**—Shorthand notation can be indicated by (1:1).

- **One-to-many**—Shorthand notation can be indicated by (1:M) or (1:N).

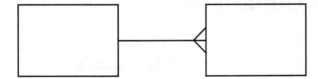

- **Many-to-many**—Shorthand notation can be indicated by (M:N) or (N:M).

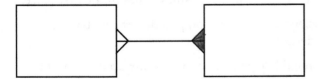

Terminology: Logical Design (ERD) versus Physical Implementation

Different but related terms are used in the "design" and "physical" realms of databases. There are close parallels between these terms, which may help you visualize the conceptual design of a database. This is analogous to looking at a construction blueprint and being able to "see" the finished project in your mind. In summary:

- **Entities** correspond to database **tables.**
- **Attributes** correspond to database **fields** in a table.
- **Key attributes** correspond to **primary keys.**

Special Considerations When Creating an ERD

- **Consider how time changes the relationship between entities.** The relationship likely changes if you consider the business rules over a week, month, or year. Avoid determining a relationship by examining only a specific point-of-time snapshot of the company. You will possibly determine the wrong relationship by doing so.
- **Clearly define entities.** Often, we use the same words to describe entities, but we mean something slightly different. Ensure that you always have a clear mutual understanding of what is meant by the name of an entity. Otherwise, you might end up again with the wrong relationships. One good way to eliminate confusion is to create a few sample records that illustrate the data to be stored in the table.
- **Identify all exceptions to the rule.** Business rules have exceptions, and you will need to really dig to find out what these are. These are often difficult to identify even if you are the business expert. Be diligent and do your best!

Relational Database Design Guidelines

- Poor relational database design leads to system failure.
- You must become a business expert in the company before you can build the company a database system.
- Proper database design accurately reflects the organization's business rules. To reinforce the previous point, you must be a business expert to understand the business rules in the first place.
- Relational database design is both an art and science. The more you practice, the better you will become as you see common patterns in many designs.
- Avoid data redundancy. Only your primary/foreign key pairings should show up in multiple entities.

Database Relationship Simplification Rules

Once your ERD is complete, you can create the database tables by applying these rules to each of the relationships. These rules ensure all relationships simplify to 1:N.

- 1:1—Relationships merge into one table. One entity becomes an attribute of the other.

- 1:N—Add primary key from the "one" entity as a foreign key in the "many" entity.

- M:N—Add intersection table that includes primary keys from both tables. Here are detailed steps for simplifying a M:N relationship.

  - Add intersection table.

  - Flip relationship lines around so "many" side faces the intersection table.

  - Add primary keys from original tables as fields in the intersection table.

  - Assign a name the intersection table.

  - Add other relevant fields to intersection table if necessary.

INDEX

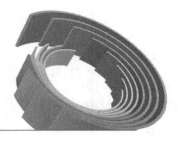

U

Unbound control, 21
Update, 34
User-friendly database system, 69–83
  alternative menu system, 70
  applied exercise, 79–81
  AutoLookup, 69
  guided exercise, 72–79
  guided exercise questions, 83
  macro, 71
  other database settings, 71
  Switchboard, 70

V

Validation Rule, 11
Validation Text, 11

X

XHTML compliance, 135

Y

Yes/No, 10